HINDU
Myths

THE • LEGENDARY • PAST

HINDU
Myths

A. L. DALLAPICCOLA

Published in co-operation with
BRITISH MUSEUM PRESS
UNIVERSITY OF TEXAS PRESS, AUSTIN

For Loredana, Leila, Dario, Roccia and in memory of
Sigrid Frances Nettekoven Melissari (1903-2002)

ACKNOWLEDGMENTS
A special thanks to Richard Blurton of The British Museum,
Department of Asia, for his unflinching and enthusiastic support.

Anna L. Dallapiccola has asserted her right
to be identified as the Author of this Work

First University of Texas Press Edition 2003
International Standard Book Number 0-292-70233-7
Library of Congress Control Number 2003110034

Requests for permission to reproduce material from this work should
be sent to Permissions, University of Texas Press, PO Box 7819, Austin, Texas 78713-7819

Designed by Martin Richards
Cover designed by Jim Stanton
Typeset in 10.25 Sabon
Printed in Great Britain by Ebenezer Baylis & Son

FRONTISPIECE: *Sandstone sculpture of Ganesha,
central India, thirteenth century.*

CONTENTS PAGE: *View of Bhutanatha Temple at
Badami, Karnataka, seventh to eleventh century.*

Contents

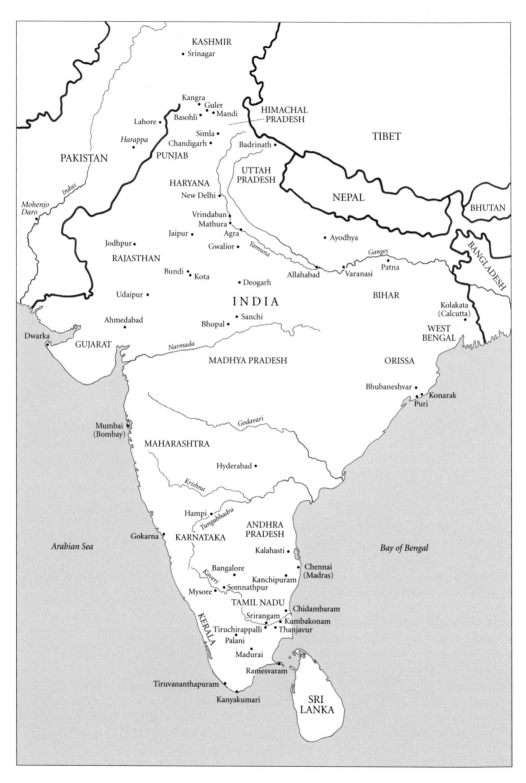

Introduction

Roughly the size of Europe, from the Atlantic Ocean to the Urals, the Indian subcontinent is home to peoples of various backgrounds, speaking different languages and following their own religious and cultural traditions. To claim that almost each state of this vast country is a land in its own right is no exaggeration. The cohesive force uniting the Hindu majority is a social structure firmly grounded in shared religious beliefs and ethic principles expressed in a wealth of myths, which form the backbone of Hindu religion and culture.

Vedic religion

Some of the earliest vestiges of religious traditions in the Indian subcontinent are cult figurines dated in the middle of the third millennium BC. These were found at Mohenjo Daro and Harappa in present day Pakistan, two of the most important sites associated with the Indus Civilization. Some scholars link these figurines of goddesses, animals, trees and sexual emblems to the beginnings of Hindu religion.

In the middle of the second millennium BC the Indus Civilization declined, probably under the brunt of the gradual penetration of the Aryans who expanded over the whole of the northern part of the subcontinent.

The lack of archaeological evidence for a distinctive Aryan civilization is compensated by an abundant literary heritage. The Aryans, credited with the introduction of Sanskrit, the sacred language of Indian scriptures, composed the four *Vedas* or '[books of] knowledge'. These collections of hymns celebrate a number of gods, some of whom eventually found their way into present-day Hinduism. Most of the Vedic gods personified natural phenomena such as the dawn, rain, fire or thunder. Vedic religion, also known as Brahmanism, was based on elaborate sacrificial rituals which were performed exclusively by Brahmin priests. Every word of these ceremonies had to be uttered following the appropriate intonation and every movement was charged with mystical meaning. There were no temples or images. Instead, the cult focused around the sacrificial altar, whose elaborate structure mirrored that of the universe. Sacrifices were vitally important because they reinvigorated the gods who, in turn looked after the well being of mankind.

Of pivotal importance was the social order. Through birth an individual belonged to one of the four castes (*varna*, colour), at whose top were the Brahmins, the only ones with access to the Vedic lore and the authority to perform rituals on behalf of the other classes: the warriors (*kshatriyas*), the agricultural workers and traders (*vaishyas*), and the menial classes (*shudras*).

During the first millennium other important texts were composed: the *Upanishads*, focusing on philosophy, and the *Brahmanas*, commentaries to the involved Vedic rituals. The two great Indian epics, the *Ramayana* and the *Mahabharata*, followed. Their cores probably date from around the sixth to fourth century BC, but reached their present form much later in the early centuries AD.

The foundation of Hinduism

In time, the Vedic creed spread to a substantial part of the subcontinent and gradually came into contact with local cults of goddesses, trees, snake deities and many others. The result was a cross-fertilization of ideas and religious practices which had a lasting impact on later developments. Between the sixth and the fifth centuries BC, two movements which were extremely critical of Vedic religion, Jainism and Buddhism, attracted a considerable number of followers and evolved to become two of the major Indian religions. In the centuries immediately preceding the Christian era, two new religious traditions emerged, one focusing on the god Vishnu (Vaishnavism) and the other on Shiva (Shaivism). Although goddesses had been venerated all along, a well-defined pattern of goddess worship emerged between the eighth and ninth centuries AD. The Great Goddess was viewed as the energy permeating the totality of the universe. All these cults promoted devotion (*bhakti*) and an unquestioning self-surrender to a chosen deity (*ishtadevata*). Contemporary Hinduism is firmly grounded on these principles. Only through devotion will one lead a meaningful life and eventually break the cycle of rebirth (*samsara*).

Hindu mythology

An innumerable and varied throng of characters populates Hindu mythology. Some have their origins in Vedic lore, such as the eight gods ruling over the eight cardinal directions (*ashtadikpalas*, the eight guardians of the sky). Among them are Indra, lord of the rain, and Agni, lord of the fire (who respectively became the guardians of the east and the south-east), Surya, the sun and Ushas, the goddess of dawn. Some developed complex characters reflecting their local origins and successive adoption into the Hindu pantheon. Others, especially goddesses, are rooted in folk religion along with spirits (*bhutas*), goblins (*ganas*) and the snake-deities (*nagas*) all dwelling in remote places. The main deities are surrounded by an 'extended family' and a host of minor figures including ascetics and sages (*rishis*), divine musicians (*gandharvas*), heavenly beauties and divine courtesans (*apsaras*) and an unspecified number of semi-divine beings, all of whom happily meddle in human affairs. This varied and vibrant cast of characters inspired innumerable myths that are narrated in the *Puranas*, 'old [stories]'.

Pan-Indian Puranas and local Puranas

These Sanskrit texts were compiled over centuries and can be defined as an encylopaedia of Hindu lore. The oldest possibly date from the early centuries AD and the most recent texts from around the sixteenth century.

Written mainly in verse, the text usually takes the form of a dialogue between a sage and a group of disciples whose questions anticipate those of the devotees. Ideally, the contents of a *Purana* should emulate a template consisting of creation, destruction and recreation, genealogies of the gods, sages and kings, the cosmic cycles and the history of various dynasties. However, this is not always the case. The narratives are interspersed with all kinds of varied theological, philosophical, scientific, ritual and astrological information. Of particular relevance to current Hindu religious practice are sections such as those dealing with the merits acquired by performing various rituals and undertaking pilgrimages. Some *Puranas* contain lengthy sections on iconography, sculpture and temple building.

There are eighteen major and eighteen minor *Puranas* and their significance in the formation of Hinduism cannot be over-emphasized. Puranic lore was the only means of disseminating religious and ethical principles among the illiterate majority as well as those who were prohibited from having access to Vedic tradition, such as women and lower-class communities.

A particularly important by-product of this literary genre are the numerous *sthalapuranas*, accounts of the mythical origins of a sacred site (*sthala*) where a deity would manifest itself or some mythological incident would occur. Although most of the legends are rooted in the classic *Puranas*, the local tradition plays a major role in their development. One of the functions, and perhaps the most important, is that of connecting a place with a mythological incident, so that the latter arguably becomes a tangible reality. These works, written either in corrupt Sanskrit or in one of the many local languages, are of vital importance for the study and appreciation of the history and religious traditions of local temples.

Important deities

Vishnu

Vishnu (all-pervading), also known as the 'preserver', epitomises stability, law and order, and is generally depicted as a heavenly king who periodically descends to earth under different aspects to redress the balance between good and evil powers. He is said to be present in all kings, who are thus expected to protect and uphold the sacred law (*dharma*). Vishnu's two wives are Bhudevi the Earth goddess and Lakshmi (good or bad sign), also known as Shri Lakshmi, the goddess of wealth and abundance. His vehicle is the divine eagle Garuda (devourer). There is a second aspect to Vishnu: when he floats on his serpent couch on the primeval waters he symbolizes release (*moksha*). Creation emanates from him effortlessly: it is only one episode in an eternal cycle of creations without beginning or end. The world, which seems so permanent

These magnificently arrayed figures show Vishnu 'the preserver' flanked by his consorts Shri-Lakshmi and Bhudevi, respectively the goddess of beauty and wealth, and the earth goddess. Bronze, Tamil Nadu, c. AD 1000.

BELOW: Gaja Lakshmi. Two elephants bathe the goddess Lakshmi seated on a lotus, and two other elephants fill their pitchers in the water. The four-armed goddess carries a lotus in her right hand; the left rests on her lap while she wrings her wet hair with the other pair. Opaque watercolour on paper, Bundi, c. 1780.

and stable is a mere bubble on the surface of the ocean. Equally, when the time comes, Vishnu becomes the destroyer of the universe. At the end of a cosmic cycle he reabsorbs the world and recycles it prior to a new creation.

Shiva

One of the most paradoxical personalities among Hindu deities is Shiva (auspicious) in whom the contrasting duties of ascetic and householder come together. As the great master of yoga he renounces the world and engages in lengthy periods of meditation. With matted hair adorned with snakes, wearing necklaces of skulls and intoxicated with hemp (*bhang*), he frequents burning grounds in the company of his host of attendants, the *ganas*. He dwells at the periphery of civilization and beckons man out of the fetters of the established order to attain the ultimate goal of release. He is also the master of music, the lord of dance, the seducer of the wives of the ascetics, and the husband of Parvati (daughter of the mountain). His two sons (both born in miraculous circumstances) are the elephant-headed Ganesha (the lord of the *ganas*), one of the most popular Hindu gods, and the six-headed Karttikeya. Shiva's vehicle is the white bull Nandi (rejoicing).

Shiva's most popular symbol, through which he is revered in most of his temples, is the *linga* or phallus, which is traditionally set in a pedestal symbolizing the *yoni* or female generative organ.

This represents the notion that Shiva is the very sap of existence. His vigour penetrates and pervades the whole of creation to bring it to life. Another popular image of Shiva is Nataraja, the 'Lord of the dance', expressing five supreme powers. He is creator, destroyer, preserver of the universe, an agent for the concealment and unveiling of truth and also a bestower of grace. Shiva, like Vishnu, is completely indifferent to the fate of his own creation. As he danced the world into being at the beginning of a creative cycle, so at the end, his dance of destruction will reduce it to ash.

Shiva and his consort. The seated couple look lovingly at each other, surrounded by a crowd of gods, divine attendants and devotees. On the pedestal are the bull Nandi and the goddess's lion. Schist, Konarak, Orissa, thirteenth century.

Devi

The great goddess has innumerable aspects that can be divided into two main categories: the nourishing, gracious and protective, or the fierce, malevolent and destructive. Devi can be depicted as a youthful, voluptuous woman such as in her aspects of Amba (the mother), Jagaddhatri (the sustainer of the world), and Annapurna (replete with food). Alternatively she is the

The goddess Kali, with dishevelled hair and protruding tongue, dressed in a skirt of hands and wearing a garland of severed heads, tramples on recumbent Shiva. Coloured print, Bengal, c. first decade of the twentieth century.

Brahma, the 'creator', carries in his upper hands a water pot and a rosary, the lower left rests on the hip, and the lower right is likely to have held a book but is now damaged. Granite, Tamil Nadu, early eleventh century.

redoubtable warrior goddess Durga (of difficult access), whose mount is a lion or a tiger, or Kali (the black) who personifies decay, destruction and death. Her gaunt aspect, protruding ribs, lolling tongue, dishevelled hair and bulging eyes graphically express the frailty and transience of human life and the necessity of transcendence through release from the entanglements of delusion (*maya*). One of Devi's main activities is to preserve and protect creation from the onslaught of demonic forces.

Brahma

Brahma is celebrated as the agent of creation in late Vedic texts but he changes character in Puranic mythology, losing much of his importance. Although still concerned with creation, his main function is as the stabilizing force between the centripetal power of Vishnu and the centrifugal figure of Shiva. He is generally depicted with four heads representing the four Vedas which, according to the legend, emanated from his four mouths. His wife is Sarasvati (the flowing-one), goddess of speech. His vehicle is the *hamsa* or goose.

Other divine beings

Ascetics and sages play a leading role in Hindu myths. Through their spiritual powers, which are acquired in years of severe austerities, they are endowed with supernatural faculties. Some are renowned for being difficult, with many gods and humans suffering the dire consequences of their wrath.

Among the most famous are Agastya (the mover of the mountain), a celebrated sage and hero of many legends. One of his greatest feats is the colonization of Southern India and the invention of the Tamil language. Another

This inspired sculpture depicts Shiva as 'Lord of the Dance' performing the dance of bliss which is said to have taken place at Chidambaram. Bronze, Thanjavur District, Tamil Nadu, c. AD 1100.

holy character is the notoriously short-tempered ascetic, Durvasas (ill-clad), reputed to be a portion of Shiva. Famous for their inquisitive minds are Markandeya (the descendant of Mrikanda) and Narada (giver of advice). Both sages were granted a glimpse into the mysteries of Vishnu's power of delusion. Narada, however, is famous for being the chief of the heavenly musicians and a gossip-monger. No less of consequence are the two rival ascetics Vasishtha (owner of wealth) and Vishvamitra (universal friend), who play a prominent role in a number of myths.

There is a continuous and unresolved conflict between the gods and their antagonists; the anti-gods (*asuras*), descendants of Diti (*daityas*) and descendants of Danu (*danavas*). They reside in splendid cities in the nether world and represent negative forces which are inevitably part of creation. A recurrent motif of many myths is how an antagonist is able to threaten the gods by the power of his austerities and trick them into granting some special favour which initially jeopardizes divine power. After numerous near misses, the gods are finally able to re-establish the balance of power and their rivals lose.

Sources of the myths

Paradoxically, India, the land of myths *par excellence*, has no equivalent in any of its numerous languages for the word myth. Myths permeate the totality of Indian culture, mementoes of mythical events dot the whole country, old myths are told anew and new myths are created. The problem faced by all who attempt the narration of select Hindu myths is which to omit. Each story is connected to many more, one more exciting than the previous; each merges in an ocean of stories.

Most of these narratives are drawn from Sanskrit literature such as the classic *Puranas* and the epics. Some myths, such as the life stories of the two Shaiva saints Kannappa and Karaikkal Ammaiyar, are taken from the *Periya Puranam*, a twelfth-century Tamil work. The stories, connected with specific temples or places, come mainly from Tamil and Kannada sources.

It should be noted that the same myth may appear in different *Puranas* and also in some *sthalapuranas*. As is to be expected, the narrative differs, emphasizing different aspects of the story according to the philosophical tradition followed by the compiler.

Organization of the book

The most famous of Indian images today, created over one thousand years ago in south India, is Shiva Nataraja, the 'Lord of the Dance'. It is a visualization of the five divine activities. It was this powerful image that inspired the division of this book into five headings: creation, preservation, destruction, the power of delusion and the bestowal of grace, the five activities shared by all Hindu deities. Within each of these chapters the myths are briefly outlined in the introductory paragraph before a fuller narration.

The ever-new beginning

Despite the remarkable ease with which India has adjusted to the quick pace of modern life in a very short period, the mythical past has not yet been forgotten.

It is clear that some of the myths' details have become slightly blurred over the centuries, and that local variations on a pan-Indian theme have emerged. The fact remains, however, that the legendary past is still living throughout the rich and varied texture of Indian everyday life. One of the best examples of this continuity is visible in the legends connected with holy places, temples and specific images, which dot the whole of the subcontinent and create a mythical network, a sacred geography, as it were.

Shiva as Adikumbeshvara

Some Hindu temples may enshrine a particular image of supernatural origin. This may be a *linga* (sign, gender, the symbol of Shiva), as in the temple in Kumbakonam known as the Adikumbeshvara (Primeval Lord of the Pot). This is the most important temple in the ancient and vibrant town of Tamil Nadu. The story connected with this temple celebrates both the renewal of creation after the periodic dissolution of the universe and Shiva in his form as Adikumbeshvara. The pot (*kumbha*) is a symbol of fertility, like the golden egg or the womb, the receptacle containing the germs of all animate and inanimate creation in the universe. In a certain sense, the pot itself becomes in the popular imagination the universe, full of potentialities.

The story tells how, when the time of the great conflagration and subsequent flood marking the end of one aeon (*kalpa*) was near, Brahma approached Shiva, asking him how the world might be created anew. Shiva instructed him to mix some earth with the nectar of immortality (*amrita*), fashion a golden pot and put in it the *Vedas* and the seeds of creation. Accordingly, Brahma made the pot, decorated it as usual with auspicious leaves, put it into a net bag and entrusted it to the water. There it was tossed by waves and pushed by winds until it floated southwards. In the course of its voyage, the decorative leaves fell off and became sacred places. Eventually, at the behest of a heavenly voice, the journey of the pot came to an end. Then Shiva, in the guise of a hunter, arrived and shot an arrow that broke open the pot. Out flowed the nectar of immortality and the seeds of creation. When the waters retreated, Brahma mixed earth with the nectar of immortality to fashion a *linga* and, in the presence of all gods, Shiva disappeared into it.

Shiva in the guise of a hunter prepares to aim an arrow at the pot to release the seeds of creation. Banapurishvara temple, Kumbakonam, Tamil Nadu. Mural by K.G.M. Muthu, late twentieth century.

The decorated pot containing the seeds of all creation floats on the waters. A coconut and auspicious leaves decorate the spout of the pot. Banapurishvara temple, Kumbakonam, Tamil Nadu. Mural by K.G.M. Muthu, late twentieth century.

Apart from addressing a number of recurring issues, this myth is relevant to the topography of Kumbakonam in that specific landmarks of the town are celebrated as the location of various phases of the story. For instance, a temple has been built in the place where Shiva reputedly stood to aim his arrow; drops of nectar which escaped from the pot are credited as the origin of two sacred tanks and, most important of all, the *linga* worshipped in the Adikumbeshvara temple is reputedly the one into which Shiva disappeared. Furthermore, the myth highlights the Adikumbeshvara temple in Kumbakonam as the most important among those in the neighbouring towns which were built where the decorative leaves fell.

Creation myths

The story of Adikumbeshvara, narrated in a number of *sthalapuranas* celebrating the sacredness of Kumbakonam, is not particularly original. The great conflagration, the subsequent flood, the new beginning and finally the structure of the universe are some of the great themes in Hindu sacred literature. However, the narratives reflect different views. The cosmos is said to originate

Vishnu reclines on the cosmic serpent Shesha, the goddess Shri Lakshmi near his feet. From his navel sprouts a lotus on which sits Brahma. Velinga, Ponda, Goa, Lakshmi-Narasimha temple, c. eighteenth century.

either from a primeval golden egg, Hiranyagarbha (golden egg or golden womb), floating in the cosmic waters, or from the interaction of the two eternal elements, spirit (*purusha*) and matter (*prakriti*), which are seen as progenitors of the golden egg. Or again, the cosmos emanates from a deity such as Vishnu from whose navel sprouts the lotus containing Brahma, the 'Grandfather' responsible for the creation, or from the limbs of a deity, Purusha, later identified with Brahma, the original male who represents the totality of creation. Despite their diversities, the overall aim of these accounts is to convey a grand vision of an ordered universe, conforming to the social and spiritual ideals of Hindu society.

The golden egg

Brahma is generally called the 'creator'. This is to a certain extent correct because whatever the sectarian bias of the various creation-myths it is Brahma who usually assumes a key role in the process. A very popular creation-myth describes the reputedly self-generated golden egg containing within its shell all phenomena and all the germs of the beings that will eventually populate the

The golden egg floats on the primeval waters. Opaque watercolour on paper, Basohli, Panjab Hills, Bharat Kala Bhavan, Varanasi, c. 1730.

universe, floating on the waters of the primeval ocean. At the beginning of each creative cycle Brahma is said to break this egg, from which the complete creation originates. The two halves of the shell form heaven, earth and the twenty-one regions of the cosmos. The mountains, clouds and mists originate from the inner and outer membranes of the egg, the rivers from the veins and the ocean from the fluids. In another version of the myth the egg is not broken to enable the emergence of life, instead, the totality of creation is contained within the unbroken eggshell.

The *Linga Purana* describes Shiva, in his androgynous form, setting in motion the process of creation by depositing his fiery seed in his female half. The cosmic egg born out of this union is said to float for thousands of years on the cosmic waters until the process of creation begins.

Vishnu as Narayana

One of the most famous creation-myths, occurring frequently in the visual arts, is Vishnu in his form as Narayana (moving in the waters), resting on his many-hooded serpent Shesha (the remainder [of a former creative cycle]), also known as Ananta (endless), whose coils symbolize the endless revolutions of time. The following narrative is drawn from the *Mahabharata*.

At the end of an aeon, Vishnu assumes the form of an all-consuming fire which destroys the totality of the universe. While this raging fire devours everything, a mass of clouds appears on the horizon. Breaking up into torrents of rain, they extinguish the flames and submerge everything in a vast sea of water. Then Vishnu assumes the form of Narayana and, lying on the thousand-headed serpent Shesha 'fierce-looking and resplendent like a thousand suns', falls into a deep sleep surrounded by darkness. When Narayana awakes, a new creation begins. Instantly a lotus sprouts from his navel and seated in its pericarp is the four-faced god Brahma, who sets the creative process in motion afresh.

Vishnu's incarnation as Matsya

Similarly, Vishnu appears in his first and third incarnations (*avataras*) respectively as Matsya, the fish, and Varaha, the boar, to create the necessary conditions for a new beginning. Matsya approaches King Manu, the designated

future ruler of all creatures, and prophesies the imminent dissolution of the cosmos. In anticipation of this cataclysmic event, the gods fashion a boat into which Manu loads the seeds of creation, the sun, the moon, Brahma, Vishnu himself, Bhava (a form of Shiva), the guardians of the directions, the four *Vedas*, the *Puranas*, the holy river Narmada, the great sage Markandeya and all the sciences. At the time of dissolution, as soon as the wind rises, Manu, by means of a snake, fastens the boat to the horn growing on the nose of Matsya, under whose guidance he and his charges survive the flood. When the new creation starts again he is the master of all creatures and the first Manu of the new creation-cycle.

Vishnu's incarnation as Varaha

There are numerous versions of the story of Varaha, all of which focus on the act of retrieving the earth from the depths of the primeval waters. The myth begins with an account of the flood following the dissolution of the previous creation. The gods, anxious to start the process of creation anew, concentrate their thoughts on Vishnu. Suddenly, a young boar slips out of Brahma's nostril and grows at an incredible rate until as large as a mountain. Awestruck, the gods begin to sing

Varaha balances the earth on his tusks, which he has lifted from the depths of the waters, and slays Hiranyaksha. The god carries in his hands his typical attributes: discus, conch, mace and lotus. Opaque watercolour on paper, Chamba, Panjab Hills, c. 1740.

his praise and Varaha dives into the depths searching for the earth. Eventually he finds it, lifts it on his tusks and makes his way to the surface of the water. While swimming upwards, the anti-god Hiranyaksha (golden-eyed) intercepts him and, after a fierce fight, Varaha kills him with his mace and emerges with the earth, placing it firmly on the waters, and the process of creation starts again.

The cosmic time dimension

As these myths clearly demonstrate, creation is not the 'beginning' and destruction not the 'end'. The Hindu perception of time is cyclical, completely different from Western thought in which time is perceived as linear. While for Western religions creation is a unique event, in Hindu philosophy creation is a continual re-creation: the universe periodically emerges, and after having gone through a cycle of four ages (*yugas*) of ever diminishing perfection, it bursts into an enormous fire and is eventually re-absorbed into the cosmic waters. After a period of quiescence, 'in void and gloom', creation commences afresh.

The gods themselves are not eternal. Brahma, the agent of creation, has a limited life span. When the time comes he, like everything else, disappears to eventually re-emerge.

The parade of the ants

Indian tradition recognizes different types of time: cosmic time, which concerns itself with extremely long spans such as the various ages of mankind from the beginning to end of a cycle; calendar time, in which centuries, years, months and days are measured, and astrological time, which combines both because it deals with large units of time such as the progression of the planets along their orbits and also takes account of the smallest units, such as the blinking of an eye, on which depends the accuracy of any astrological calculation.

Preoccupation with the ever-revolving cycles and aeons is a constant feature in Indian myths. This is vividly illustrated in the following famous story drawn from the *Brahma Vaivarta Purana*.

After his victory over the drought-demon Vritra, and having released the waters of the universe from captivity, the king of the gods, Indra, decided to celebrate his victory. He called the divine architect Vishvakarman and requested him to create an abode the like of which had never been seen before, fit for a king who had subjugated all his enemies. Vishvakarman began to carry out Indra's instructions, but each time a design was completed Indra ordered something grander to suit his soaring ambition. Vishvakarman grew tired of this and complained to Brahma, who then approached Vishnu, and although not openly committing himself, Vishnu indicated that this problem would be solved.

A small boy of about ten, emanating spiritual radiance, arrived at the palace and was welcomed by Indra. The child, who was none other than Vishnu in disguise, sat and asked Indra when the construction of this magnificent town would be completed, since no previous Indra had ever had such a beautiful residence. Indra was taken aback by the notion of previous Indras and probed the child's knowledge. The child explained the sequence of the ages of mankind, those of the universe and the various Indras and Vishvakarmans which had previously existed. Furthermore, the child explained, there are multiple universes, each with a Brahma, Shiva and Vishnu, and that each would disappear with no knowledge of any simultaneous existence elsewhere. In essence, what will come has already existed. The child fell silent, but smiled as a huge procession of ants appeared. He explained the thousands of ants were the previous Indras, all of which rose and fell in status because of their *karma*. Then an elderly ascetic (Shiva in an assumed form) entered and began explaining his decision to engage in spiritual endeavours rather than marriage. On his chest was a tuft of hair: its core had disappeared and only the outer ring of hair remained. For each Brahma which had died, a hair fell from his chest. Suddenly both the child and the elderly man disappeared, and Indra, shaken by the transience of existence, realized there was little to life. He announced an end to building, for what had been achieved was sufficient.

On the one hand, the message of the myth is the cyclical notion of time and, on the other, the simultaneous existence of many universes. Nothing is really unique, all things come, go and return.

The four ages of mankind

From the beginning of a universe to its conflagration, the 'history' of mankind is divided into four ages. Each is preceded and followed by a relatively short period called *sandhya* (twilight) and *sandhyamsha* (part of twilight). The first of the ages of mankind is the Krita or Satya, the most perfect of all eras, which lasts 4800 divine years (a divine year lasts 360 human years). During this time everyone follows the tenets of the cosmic and sacred law (*dharma*). Mankind

enjoys a long and carefree life. Religious observances and social order are scrupulously observed. The cosmic and sacred law is represented by a bull, standing firmly and on his four legs.

The following age of Treta lasts a total of 3600 divine years. During this time the first hints of decay seep into the universe and the bull stands on three legs.

The third age, Dvapara, is even shorter than the preceding, lasting

The thousand-eyed Indra, guardian of the east, armed with two thunderbolts in the upper hands and an elephant goad in the lower right, sits on his elephant, Airavata. Opaque watercolour on paper, Thanjavur (?), Tamil Nadu, c. 1830.

2400 divine years in which the inexorable process of deterioration continues with the bull reduced to standing on two legs. The fourth is the present age of Kali, the shortest of all, with its mere 1200 divine years, in which moral standards have sunk to the lowest possible ebb. The bull of *dharma* precariously balances his weight on one leg alone.

The aeons

This cycle of four ages lasts 4,320,000 human years and is called a *mahayuga* or 'great age'. One thousand 'great ages' make an aeon (*kalpa*), consisting of one day in the life of a Brahma, with the night of equal duration. The life of a Brahma lasts one hundred years of the gods. Creation, however, lasts only a day of a Brahma, which is divided into fourteen ages, each presided over by its own Manu, its own set of gods, sages and kings. A Manu is a semi-divine being, reputed to be the ancestor of a number of ruling dynasties and, most important of all, the originator and upholder of the traditional social order.

The present day of Brahma is called the Varaha *kalpa* because during this cycle Vishnu assumes the form of a boar; we are in the age of the seventh Manu, Vaivasvata, the progenitor of the human race, the very Manu who played a pivotal role in the fish incarnation of Vishnu and, as such, is a sort of Indian Noah.

Dissolution and re-creation of the universe

At the end of a Manu's reign creation dissolves in what could be called a partial dissolution (*pralaya*), followed by a period of rest before the process of generation renews. Complete dissolution (*mahapralaya*) occurs at the end of the life of a Brahma when all the elements constituting the universe are re-absorbed into the body of the creator. Then, again after a period of quiescence, the creator feels the impulse to create anew and the cycle starts again.

The creation emanates from Brahma

As already mentioned, Brahma is directly responsible for creation: he either breaks the golden egg, or dwells in it, or sprouts along with the lotus flower from Vishnu's navel.

A recurring theme is the crucial role played by the three qualities or principles (*gunas*) which determine the character of all created beings. The shining purity (*sattva*) is characteristic of the divine beings, the dynamic passion (*rajas*) is the predominant quality in mankind, and the dark inertia (*tamas*) defines the antagonists (*asuras*) of the gods. These three principles are often identified with the gods Brahma, Vishnu and Shiva-Rudra, who are responsible for the creation, preservation and destruction of the universe. Each deity represents one of these three principles, which together form primeval or gross matter, the source of the material world.

According to the account of the *Vishnu Purana*, creation emanated from Brahma's body. Furthermore, while he was intent on creating the world, beings endowed with purity emerged from his mouth; beings endowed with passion and strength emerged from his chest; others filled with both passion and inertia sprang from his thighs; and finally, from his feet came those filled with inertia.

These form the four traditional castes of Hindu society: Brahmins, *kshatriyas*, *vaishyas* and *shudras*; each was created for the observance and performance of duties which carry particular importance. The passage expresses one of the crucial principles of Hindu religion: gods and mankind are interdependent. The gods are nourished by sacrifices while mankind is supported by rain sent by the gods.

The cosmos and its structure

The majority of texts enter into elaborate and varied descriptions of the cosmos and its inhabitants: gods, humans, semi-divine beings, chthonian divinities, ghosts and goblins, to name but a few.

Three zones or localities (*triloka*) constitute the universe. Each of these is subdivided into seven regions, so the entire cosmos comprises twenty-one different regions. The first of these is simply called 'zone' (*loka*) and contains the sphere of the gods, the atmosphere, the earth, the heavens of various deities, immortal beings, the sun, the moon and the planets. The heavenly bodies are thought to be connected by invisible ropes of wind to the pole star, Dhruva (fixed, unswerving), the centre around which they revolve. The sun and moon are imagined as sitting in chariots, drawn respectively by a seven-headed horse and gazelles. The sun rotates around Mount Meru, thus determining the rhythm of night and day. The waxing and waning of the moon is due to the need of various inhabitants of heaven to drink the nectar, which is poured into the moon by the sun. Once the nectar reserves diminish, the moon wanes, and when filled anew by the sun it waxes. Eclipses are caused by Rahu, a demon who is represented as a head without a body, who chases the moon before eating it. However, soon after being devoured, it re-emerges from Rahu's neck (p.30).

The second zone is called 'place' (*tala*). Sited immediately below the earth, it is inhabited by chthonian divinities such as the snakes, various categories of anti-gods (*asuras, daityas, danavas*), and numerous types of ghosts and goblins, all of whom play prominent roles in mythology. These creatures are not necessarily malevolent, but may become dangerous if not shown due respect by mankind. The netherworld, contrary to what one would expect, is the home of some of the most splendid regions of the cosmos. Of prominence is the world of the snake-deities, the Patala. Its capital, Bhogavati (the abode of enjoyment), where the streets are paved with precious gems, is described in glowing terms in a number of texts. The same is true of the realms of the anti-gods, all of whom live in splendid mansions with gardens and pleasure groves, leading lives of luxury.

The third zone, beneath the netherworld, is hell (*naraka*), where sinners are punished. The traditional number of regions which constitute hell is seven, but this varies according to the texts. There is an ample repertoire of punishments meted out to sinners. For instance, those who sowed dissension between friends, between husband and wife, between brothers, are sawn in two; huge birds pick the tongues from the mouths of slanderers while hurling insults at them; those who treated parents and teachers contemptuously will lie with their face immersed in pus, faeces and urine; those who touched a fire, a cow or a Brahmin in a state of impurity will be thrust in the hell called 'burning vat';

those who urinated before cows, Brahmins, the sun or a fire will have their intestines ripped out through the anus by crows; those who had intercourse on festive days or who committed adultery will embrace an incandescent, pointed spike. Others are condemned to eat polluted things such as dogs, scorpions and excrement or to carry millstones around their necks; there is no end to the list of gruesome descriptions. As time is cyclical, however, the sojourn in hell as well as in heaven is temporary, and is eventually succeeded by rebirth.

Puranic cosmography

The majority of *Puranas* give a detailed description of the various worlds of the gods, the ancestors and mankind.

The sacred mountain, Meru, marking the centre of a complex scheme, rises in the middle of the celestial regions. At its summit live Brahma, Shiva and Vishnu along with gods, goddesses, sages and semi-divine beings. In the eight directions of space (four main and four intermediate points of the compass) are the capitals of the eight guardians of space. The river Ganga (the Ganges) falls from the heavens, directly on Mount Meru and, after flowing around the city of the gods, it branches in different directions, one of which traverses Jambudvipa (Island of the rose-apple tree), the south portion of which is Bharat, India.

Beneath Mount Meru are the seven concentric island-continents constituting the world. Jambudvipa, the central island, is identified with the earth. Each of the seven island-continents is divided from the next by a sea of sugar-cane juice, wine, clarified butter, curds, milk and fresh water. Across this last stretch of sea is the fabulous land Lokaloka (world-no-world), which delimits the visible world from the world of darkness. Beyond this is the outer shell of the cosmic egg, enclosing the whole cosmos.

Aja-ekapada (one-footed goat) holds the earth and sky apart. The earth is flat and rests on the hood of the cosmic serpent Shesha, which is supported in turn by the primeval tortoise Akupara, whose four feet rest on the elephants standing on the shell of the cosmic egg at the bottom of the abyss. The first divine elephant to emerge from the shell of the cosmic egg in Brahma's right hand was Airavata, followed by seven other elephants. From the shell in Brahma's left hand emerged eight female elephants. These eight couples are reputed to be the progenitors of all elephants living on earth and in the sky, and it is they who support the cosmos from their places in the four main and four intermediate directions of space.

These narratives have been retold over many centuries with additions and variations. Hindu thought is preoccupied with a finely structured hierarchical order of the universe in which all the categories of beings are neatly accommodated to provide a template for human society. Furthermore, the whole cosmos is an integrated system, and every creature, whether animate or inanimate, plays a vital role within it.

Preservation

The process of creation did not proceed as smoothly as might have been expected; from its inception the rivals of the gods kept a keen eye on the proceedings. This unresolved conflict between the gods and their antagonists, who appear in different guises during the ever-revolving cycle of time, is one of the central themes permeating the myths. The gods are forced to acknowledge the power of their devotees, be they humans, animals or anti-gods, by fulfilling their wishes. For the most part it is the wishes of the devotees which eventually limit or destroy the power of the gods. The latter devise ruses that, at a given moment, will retort against their adversaries. But it is not only the anti-gods who pose a threat, more frequently the danger arises from humans, the redoubtable seers or sages, charged with tremendous power accumulated during long years of severe asceticism. These formidable characters play a crucial role, in both a positive and negative sense, in much of Hindu mythology.

Vishnu's descents (*avataras*)

Although all Hindu gods have the power to create, preserve and destroy, the god usually associated with the preservation of the cosmic order is Vishnu 'the all-pervading'. He repeatedly rescues creation from the brink of catastrophe by means of his periodic incarnations or, more precisely, his 'descents', during which he re-establishes the balance between good and evil.

According to Vishnu's devotees, his incarnations are innumerable. Although usually ten, they are occasionally twelve, or twenty two. The traditional list of ten comprises Matsya (fish), Kurma (tortoise), Varaha (boar), Narasimha (man-lion), Vamana (dwarf), Parashurama (Rama with the axe), Ramachandra (Rama-the-Moon), Balarama (Rama-the-Strong), Krishna (Black, or Dark-One) and finally Kalki (having a white horse), which will appear at the end of the current Kali age, ushering in the process of dissolution. Not all Vaishnavas consider Balarama an incarnation; sometimes he is omitted and the Buddha takes his place. As opinions differ on the number of incarnations, so does the amount of detail within the accounts.

Matsya and Varaha are connected with myths of creation. Manu's boat contains the potential of creation which Matsya tows through the flood, and Varaha rescues the earth from the depths of the waters by killing Hiranyaksha.

Vishnu's incarnation as a tortoise

The second incarnation is Kurma, the tortoise, and the myth illustrates one of the recurrent motifs in Hindu lore, the acquisition of supernatural power through penance and meditation. The account of Vishnu's incarnation shows Brahma, Shiva and Vishnu jointly engaged with the anti-gods in retrieving the nectar of immortality from the depths of the Ocean of Milk. The myth incorporates a number of themes other than the power of asceticism. These include the decline of divine power, the continuing battle between gods and their rivals, and the victory of the gods through Vishnu's intervention.

From a Vaishnava point of view this myth is the celebration of the all-pervasiveness of Vishnu. He is shown not only as Kurma supporting Mount Mandara, but also in human form, sitting on its summit in full control, and thirdly with the other gods pulling the churning rope. An important detail in the myth is that among the auspicious things retrieved from the Ocean of Milk is Vishnu's future wife, the radiant Shri-Lakshmi (prosperity, wealth, beauty) who, after casting a critical gaze on the gods, chooses Vishnu as her spouse. The following account is drawn from the *Vishnu Purana*.

The gods' power dwindled rapidly because of an unfortunate meeting between Indra and the notoriously ill-tempered ascetic Durvasas, who was none other than a portion of Shiva. The story tells how Durvasas was living in a forest engaged in meditation, when a beautiful nymph presented him with a splendid garland of flowers. The sage placed the garland on his head and resumed his spiritual activities, which required him to behave in a frenzied manner. By chance Indra arrived, seated on his elephant Airavata, and Durvasas threw the garland around the elephant's head. The elephant became inebriated by the garland's heavenly perfume and threw it to the ground, at which Durvasas took offence and cursed Indra.

At this, Indra lost his strength. Trees and plants withered and died; sacrifices were no longer offered to the gods, and a crisis of untold magnitude loomed. Taking advantage of this, the anti-gods decided to pitch their strength against the gods and overpower them. Indra and the rest, divested of their splendour, fled to Brahma and together they explained their precarious situation to Vishnu, who promised to restore their power and strength. He devised a shrewd plan, by which the gods, together with the anti-gods, would throw all sorts of medicinal herbs into the Ocean of Milk. Then they would use Mount Mandara as a churning stick and the great king of the serpents, Vasuki, as a rope, and with his help they would churn the Ocean and obtain the nectar of immortality. Yet there was a problem. The gods had first to make peace and secure the assistance of their enemies. The terms were agreed that once the nectar emerged, it would be equally shared between the gods and their antagonists. Vishnu, however, promised the perplexed gods that not a single drop of nectar would fall into the hands of their rivals.

Immediately all sides were pacified and began to work, selecting medicinal herbs and throwing them in the depths of the Ocean of Milk. They then uprooted Mount Mandara to be the staff and the serpent Vasuki volunteered as the cord, but an argument ensued as to who should take the serpent by the tail

LEFT: *The tortoise incarnation of Vishnu. In the upper pair of hands the god carries a discus and conch. The lower ones are in the reassuring and boon-giving gesture. Opaque watercolour on paper, Thanjavur (?), Tamil Nadu, c. 1830.*

OPPOSITE: *The churning of the Ocean of Milk. Vishnu as tortoise supports Mount Mandara, the churning stick, while the snake Vasuki is the rope pulled by the gods and their rivals. In the background are the various objects retrieved from the ocean. Opaque watercolour on paper, Maharashtra (?), c. 1800.*

and who by the head. Vishnu persuaded the gods to grasp the tail, while the anti-gods held the head and the neck. When churning had begun, terrible fumes and a scorching heat rose from the hoods of Vasuki, overpowering the anti-gods. Simultaneously, his breath drove clouds towards his tail which revived the gods with a refreshing rain. Noticing that Mandara was unstable, Vishnu assumed the form of a tortoise and dived into the Ocean to serve as a pivot for the mountain. He was also present in other forms, helping the gods to pull the mighty Vasuki, and sitting upon the mountain and allowing one portion of his divine energy to enter and sustain the serpent, while another entered the gods.

The Ocean yielded many gifts, the first being the cow Surabhi, the 'fountain of milk and curds'; then came the goddess of wine, Varuni, whose eyes were 'rolling with intoxication'; the heavenly *parijata* tree and lovely divine courtesans followed; the moon surfaced from the depths and was immediately seized by Mahadeva (Shiva); when the poison had been generated by the sea it was taken by the snake-deities; Dhanvantari, the physician of the gods, surfaced next with the cup of nectar, followed by the goddess Shri-Lakshmi seated on a lotus in full bloom. The great sages, heavenly choirs and divine courtesans, welcomed her. The Ganga and other rivers bathed her. The Ocean presented her with a garland of never-fading flowers, and the divine architect, Vishvakarman, fashioned her priceless jewels. Once bathed and attired, she chose Vishnu as her husband and reclined on his chest, casting her auspicious gaze upon the deities. But, as Vishnu turned away, the incensed anti-gods snatched the cup of nectar from the hands of Dhanvantari. Vishnu, however, assumed the form of a beautiful woman, charming them with sidelong glances and an alluring figure until

he recovered the vessel. As soon as the gods began to drink, their rivals fell upon them with weapons but the revived gods defeated them, and the anti-gods plunged again into the netherworld. Finally the gods sang the praises of Vishnu as normality was restored.

The number of objects retrieved from the Ocean varies according to the different versions of the myth. Some narratives dwell on a number of details, such as the *Agni Purana* which explains the origin of the eclipses. Thus, when Vishnu, in his female aspect, snatched the vessel containing the nectar of

Cut into two parts by Vishnu's disc, Rahu is shown as a fierce-looking half man. The two crescents in his hands are probably the sun and the moon which he periodically devours. Schist, Konarak, Orissa, thirteenth century.

immortality from the anti-gods, one of them, Rahu, pretended to be a god and joined them. At just the moment in which he started to drink the nectar he was exposed by the sun and the moon and Vishnu decapitated him. His head, however, had become immortal, and ever since, Rahu is said to chase the sun and the moon and periodically swallow them, thereby causing eclipses.

Shiva swallows the poison

In the above version of the myth, the snake-deities seize the poison emerging from the Ocean, while in other accounts, such as the *Bhagavata Purana* and the *Kurma Purana*, Shiva drinks it to save creation from obliteration. His wife, Parvati, conscious of the mortal danger incurred by him, pressed his throat with her hand so he was unable to swallow, while Vishnu held his hands on his mouth to prevent him from spitting it out. The poison remained in Shiva's throat and burnt it blue, hence Shiva's epithet, blue-throated (Nilakantha).

Other incarnations

The fourth incarnation of Vishnu is Narasimha, the man lion, who hints at a rivalry between Shaivas and Vaishnavas. Here Vishnu descends to earth only to destroy the anti-god Hiranyakashipu (golden-robed), a staunch Shaiva, while rescuing his son, an ardent Vaishnava, from his father's persecutions (p.65). The story of Vamana the dwarf again handles the well-known theme of the anti-god, whose accumulated merits, generosity and piety threaten the supremacy of the gods. In this case the anti-god Bali is not killed, but is merely sent to rule over the netherworld.

Vishnu's human incarnations

The most famous among Vishnu's incarnations are Ramachandra (Rama-the-Moon), or simply Rama (pleasing), and Krishna who, during the course of time have become deities in their own right. These two are 'complete incarnations' in which the divine power manifests itself fully rather than partially, as is the case in the other incarnations. Furthermore, these are the only ones which span the complete cycle of human life from birth to death.

The story of Rama is given in great detail in the *Ramayana* (Rama's career), one of the two great epics of India. The mythical author of this Sanskrit work, which consists of around 96,000 verses in seven books, is reputedly the sage Valmiki. There are a number of versions which show marked regional influences, differing on many points and varying in length. The text underwent various phases of development and contains a number of interpolations, as well as the addition of the first and last books in which Rama is represented as an incarnation of Vishnu, while the core of the poem presents him as a human hero. It is uncertain when the *Ramayana* was composed, and various opinions date the core of the poem between 500 BC and AD 200.

Balakanda or 'Book of Childhood'

The myth begins with the kingdom of Kosala and its king, the mighty Dasharatha (having ten chariots), who ruled from Ayodhya in north India. The king has everything except a son and heir, and invites the renowned sage Rishyashringa (deer-horned) to perform a ritual ensuring the birth of a son. While the sage is engaged in this, a divine character emerges from the fire with a pot containing a heavenly sweetmeat for the king, which is divided among the three queens of Dasharatha. Subsequently four boys are born: Rama, Bharata, Lakshmana and Shatrughna. These receive different portions of Vishnu's divine personality because he had condescended to be reborn in order to destroy the mighty king of Lanka, Ravana (roaring). The latter had harassed the gods because he was in receipt of a favour decreeing he could only be killed by a mortal.

When the sons are barely out of childhood, the sage Vishvamitra (universal friend) appears at the court of Dasharatha and requests the king to allow his eldest and dearest son Rama to accompany him to the forest to kill the impure creatures that were disturbing his rituals. The heavy-hearted king lets Rama go, accompanied by Lakshmana (endowed with auspicious marks), who is an incarnation of Vishnu's serpent. On their way to the sage's hermitage they are taught various magic spells and familiarize themselves with myths connected to the places they pass through, thus completing their education. One of Rama's first deeds is to kill a dreadful demoness, for which Vishvamitra rewards him with a set of magical weapons which eventually enable him to dispatch the demons polluting the sage's sacrifice. Once accomplished, the trio travel to the town of Mithila, to participate in a contest organized by King Janaka to see who is able to string the divine bow and thereby marry his daughter Sita (furrow). Rama not only strings the bow, but breaks it, and marriages are arranged between the four Ayodhya princes and the daughters and

Rama seated on a hillock converses with Hanuman, while to the left, Lakshmana listens attentively. Opaque watercolour on paper, Thanjavur (?) Tamil Nadu, c. 1830.

nieces of Janaka. The marriage party sets out for Ayodhya, and on route they meet the redoubtable Brahmin Parashurama, the scourge of the warrior class, to which Rama and the others belong. Rama defeats Parashurama, and on reaching Ayodhya the party is met by welcoming crowds.

Ayodhyakanda or 'Book of Ayodhya'

The second book deals mainly with courtly intrigues which result in Rama's banishment. King Dasharatha resolves to abdicate and consecrate Rama as prince regent. Shortly before the event, the hunchback maid of the junior queen, Kaikeyi, poisons the mind of her mistress by convincing her that her son Bharata should instead be consecrated, and that she should now claim the two favours which the king had granted her previously. A dramatic scene ensues and the heart-broken Dasharatha concedes her wishes. Rama is sent on fourteen years' exile and the throne passes to Bharata. While the entire population grieves for the exiled prince, the disconsolate Dasharatha dies. Bharata, who at that time was not in town, is immediately summoned to Ayodhya but after violent discussion refuses to fulfil his mother's wishes. He then heads for the forest, hoping to convince Rama to return and rule, but Rama is determined to obey his father's command and refuses to return prior to fourteen years elapsing. Eventually, a compromise is found; Bharata rules in Rama's name and, as a symbol of Rama's power, Bharata sets his brother's sandals on Ayodhya's throne and rules from a small village near the capital. In the meantime, Rama, Lakshmana and Sita wander through the wilderness.

Aranyakanda or 'Book of the Forest'

The third book describes the adventures of the three exiles in the forests, inhabited only by stern ascetics, fierce demons and other terrifying creatures. Ravana's sister, Shurpanakha (she whose fingernails are like winnowing fans), visits the exiles in the forest with a view to seducing Rama. Her charms fail firstly with Rama, then with Lakshmana, and the scorned demoness attempts to kill Sita. In revenge Lakshmana cuts off her nose and ears until, shrieking and bleeding, she returns to her brother, the mighty Ravana, who sends an army of his followers under the command of his brother Khara to destroy

Leaf from a storyteller's book. On the left, Shurpanakha is shown making advances to Rama, and on the right, Lakshmana grabs her by the hair and cuts off her nose and ears. Opaque watercolour on paper, Maharashtra (?), nineteenth century.

Rama and Lakshmana. The expedition fails despite Khara's presence on the battlefield. When Ravana hears of Rama's victory he resolves to abduct Sita and enrols the help of his uncle, Maricha, who assumes the disguise of a gazelle and roams near the exile's hut, eventually captivating Sita's fancy. Rama sets out to capture the animal and is lured away into the depths of the forest. Despite Rama's strict orders, Lakshmana leaves Sita and follows his brother. At this moment, a mendicant, none other than Ravana, appears at Sita's door and abducts her in his aerial chariot. The gallant vulture Jatayus tries to intercept the flight of the chariot and falls to earth seriously wounded. While Sita is flown to Lanka and kept captive in Ravana's palace, Rama and Lakshmana return to find her gone. On searching, they find Jatayus who, in his dying breath, explains what has happened and directs them towards the kingdom of the monkeys, Kishkindha.

Kishkindhakanda or 'Book of Kishkindha'

The fourth book introduces a new set of characters, the 'inhabitants of the forest' (*vanaras*). The term is generally interpreted as 'monkeys', including the great monkey-hero, Hanuman (heavy-jawed), and Sugriva (having a beautiful neck), the exiled pretender to the throne of Kishkindha. Sugriva makes a pact with Rama: the hero will help him to kill his brother Valin (tailed), reconquer the throne and marry Valin's wife. Once Rama has fulfilled his part of the pact, Sugriva and the monkeys start searching for Sita. A group headed by Angada and Hanuman find Sita in Lanka with the help of Jatayus' brother. Hanuman resolves to visit her, which involves jumping across the strait dividing India from Lanka, and after marvellous adventures lands safely at Lanka's gate.

Sundarakanda or 'Beautiful Book'

The fifth book focuses on the exploits of Hanuman in Lanka. He succeeds in talking to Sita and hands her Rama's signet ring as a token of his good faith, while also using the opportunity for reconnoitring the palace grounds. In so doing he wreaks havoc in Ravana's gardens, fights against a number of guards, is taken prisoner by Ravana's son Indrajit and dragged into Ravana's presence. After a dramatic interview in which he tries in vain to convince the king to return Sita, he is freed from captivity, but as punishment his tail is set alight. Jumping from roof to roof on his way to the ocean, Hanuman sets Lanka ablaze. His return to the mainland is celebrated by his clan, and together they return to Kishkindha to report to Rama.

Yuddhakanda or 'Book of the Battle'

The sixth book centres on the battle in front of Ravana's capital. On arrival on the seashore the allies are joined by Vibhishana (frightful), one of Ravana's brothers, who, disgusted by Ravana's demeanour, defects to Rama. The monkeys build a bridge across the strait, and eventually Rama kills Ravana in a duel. Vibhishana is consecrated King of Lanka and Sita is recalled. On her arrival, Rama, instead of rejoicing, heaps abuse and disowns her because she had lived in another man's house. To prove her chastity, Sita walks into a burning pyre and remains unscathed. Only then does Rama agree to take her back, and they return to Ayodhya, where Rama is consecrated king.

Scene from a storyteller's scroll. Sita, unscathed, kneels with a garland in her hand amidst raging flames. Facing her are Rama and Lakshmana. Opaque watercolour on paper, Bishnupur, Bankura District, Bengal, mid-nineteenth century.

Uttarakanda or 'Last Book'

This book narrates the last years of Rama, Sita and his brothers. Gossip about Sita's infidelity continues to poison the atmosphere and Rama, although knowing the rumours are unfounded, obeys what he considers his duty as a ruler and banishes Sita, who is pregnant. Later, during a horse sacrifice, two handsome youths appear and begin to recite the *Ramayana*. These are the twin sons of Rama and Sita, who were born in the hermitage of the sage Valmiki, the author of the poem. Rama sends for Sita, intending to take her back, but having already suffered too much she prays to the goddess Earth, her mother, to recall her. The ground beneath her opens and she vanishes forever. Rama divides his kingdom between his sons, enters the river Sarayu and yields up his life to merge with Vishnu.

The story of Krishna

Alongside Rama, Krishna is the most widely worshipped among Vishnu's incarnations. While Rama epitomises the perfect son, brother, husband and king who follows sacred law and the path of restraint to utmost consequences, Krishna has a flamboyant and complex personality.

Although his cult probably dates back to the early centuries AD, Krishna's character has developed considerably over the course of time, incorporating traits from different deities. His life-story reveals a number of different facets; a child-god who loves playing pranks and practical jokes, and a handsome, youthful, dark-skinned pastoral god who plays the flute and has hair adorned with peacock's feathers. His oozing melodies ravish the minds and souls of the milkmaids (*gopis*). The erotic elements pervading the early phase of Krishna's story may have connections with a fertility cult. However, the relationship of Krishna and the milkmaids has been explained as representing the yearning of the individual soul to be united with the Lord. Around the tenth or eleventh century, Radha emerged from the group of milkmaids as a distinct personality and became Krishna's beloved *par excellence*. Their great love affair has constantly inspired poets and artists.

Yet another facet to Krishna's character is revealed during the moment he leaves the cowherds' settlement for Mathura and sloughs off his pastoral nature to become an accomplished ruler and statesman. He is king of the Yadavas, whose capital is Dwarka on the shores of the Arabian Sea, and also the shrewd politician and philosophical counsellor of the Pandavas, who play a pivotal role in the great Indian epic, the *Mahabharata*.

The following narrative is based on both the *Bhagavata Purana* and the *Mahabharata,* and begins with a description of the misery endured by the goddess Earth at the hands of tyrannical kings and anti-gods. She complains about the imbalance between good and evil and asks the gods to relieve her burden. Vishnu plucks two hairs, one white and one black, saying each will be reborn on earth in human form. The black hair became Krishna, the eighth child of Devaki and her husband, Vasudeva. The white hair was born as Balarama, the seventh child of the couple. Together, both would free the earth from the evil forces.

Birth of Krishna

While proceeding to the wedding of his sister Devaki to Vasudeva, Kamsa heard a celestial voice forecasting his own death by one of Devaki's children. Kamsa was prevented by Vasudeva from killing Devaki on the spot, but after the ceremony Kamsa held them captive in a well-guarded place and killed every child born to them. Six children had been killed, when the seventh was conceived, Balarama, who was a portion of Vishnu's snake Ananta. On this occasion, divine intervention transferred the embryo to the womb of Rohini, another wife of Vasudeva, who lived away from Mathura in a settlement of cowherds headed by Nanda (joy). Rohini bore the child, but Kamsa was told that Devaki had miscarried. Then Krishna too was born to her. His birth during the month of Bhadrapada (August–September), at the height of the rainy season, was heralded by a number of miraculous events. At the moment of his birth, Krishna momentarily appeared in his divine aspect to his parents. He asked Vasudeva to take him to Gokula (cow shed), a settlement across the river Yamuna, and substitute the daughter of Yashoda (conferring fame) in his place. Having requested this he resumed the aspect of a newborn child, at which moment the shackles fell from the hands and feet of Vasudeva, the dungeon doors opened, the guards and dogs fell into a deep sleep and Vasudeva, carrying the baby in a basket, walked towards the flooded river. He crossed it, entered the cowherds' hamlet and, placing Krishna beside Yashoda, who was peacefully asleep, picked up her newly-born daughter and returned to Mathura. Everything appeared as if nothing had happened. In the morning, Kamsa was told that an eighth child was born to his sister, and he took the baby by the feet and smashed its head upon a stone. At that moment the huge eight-armed figure of the Great Goddess appeared in the sky announcing to Kamsa that the one who was to kill him had been born. Without further ado, Kamsa decided to kill all the children born that day.

Krishna's childhood and youth exploits

Meanwhile, Krishna's life continued peacefully in the idyllic surroundings of Nanda's settlement until Kamsa sent a number of demons to destroy Krishna. The first was the demoness Putana (stinking-one) who, disguised as a handsome young woman, went to Yashoda's house and placed the baby Krishna on her lap. Immediately, as she placed the child at her breast, which was smeared with poison, Krishna became aware of her demonic nature and squeezed hard to suck the life from her. In turn, the demon Trinavarta arrived in the form of a whirlwind which enveloped the whole of Gokula and blinded everyone with the dust. In the confusion, Trinavarta snatched Krishna and took him high into the sky, but the infant started gaining weight and soon the huge load hampered the demon's ascent. Then Krishna throttled him until he fell to earth dead, still holding the child unscathed in his arms.

Despite numerous encounters with the envoys of Kamsa, Krishna behaved like the other boys of the settlement, pilfering the milkmaids' stores of milk, butter and curds, and playing innumerable pranks; there was no hint of his divine nature except on rare occasions. One such episode was when Krishna chose to eat mud. This was reported to Yashoda but Krishna, when quizzed, flatly denied it. Yashoda, for once genuinely angry, asked him to open his mouth and was dumbstruck to see within it the entire universe. As Krishna closed his mouth she entirely forgot the vision. This sequence of prodigious events continued to unsettle the inhabitants of Gokula, so Nanda decided to move to Vrindavana (forest of basil). By this time Krishna and Balarama were old enough to help look after the cattle and went out with the animals into the woods. Here too, they were confronted anew by a spate of troublesome creatures sent by Kamsa. The gods also chose to play tricks for the sheer pleasure of seeing another of Krishna's feats. Brahma, for instance, descended to earth and abducted and imprisoned Krishna's friends and cattle in a remote cavern. Missing them, Krishna immediately understood this to be Brahma's work. Krishna created multiples of himself which assumed the features of the missing boys and cattle, and returned to Vrindavana. Nobody suspected anything was amiss. This continued for a year, until Brahma wondered what had happened for he could see the boys and the animals roaming in the forest. Although he knew that they were not those he held captive, he was unable to tell the difference. While pondering this, they all appeared to him as Vishnu and, humbled by Vishnu's power of delusion, he prostrated himself at their feet.

Despite the threats, life continued and Krishna, now a handsome youth, charmed the milkmaids' hearts and minds both with his appearance and the music of his flute. One of the most famous episodes in this phase of his life was the theft of the milkmaids' clothes while bathing. The girls bathed in obser-

This detail from a folio of a Bhagavata Purana *manuscript shows the* rasa-*dance during which Krishna multiplied himself so that each milkmaid thought he was dancing only with her. Opaque watercolour on paper, Nathdwara, Rajasthan, c. 1770.*

vance of a ritual in the first winter month. Krishna surreptitiously took their clothes from the river bank and hid in a nearby tree from where he called the embarrassed girls to come, with their hands raised above their heads, and collect their clothes.

Soon afterwards Krishna entered into conflict with the rain god Indra. The cowherds regularly worshipped Indra, until Krishna announced that, being herdsmen and not agriculturalists, they should instead worship the nearby Mount Govardhana (increaser of cattle). On seeing this, an irate Indra unleashed a tremendous storm which lasted seven days and nights. The cowherds turned to Krishna for help; he uprooted Mount Govardhana, lifted it effortlessly, and held it on the little finger of his left hand while the cowherds and their animals took shelter beneath it. Eventually, the humbled Indra descended from the sky and offered prayers and worship to Krishna.

The magic of Krishna's flute was such that, on hearing its beautiful notes, the milkmaids became aglow with passion, leaving their husbands, children and houses and rushing to the trysting place in the forest. There are many stories narrating this phase of his life, the most important of which describes the round dance of Krishna, the *rasa-mandala*, with the milkmaids. During this dance, he multiplied himself to give the milkmaids the illusion that each of them alone was dancing with him. The message conveyed through the erotic imagery pervading this episode relates to the individual human soul which is represented by the milkmaids. Each one is irresistibly attracted to the summoning of God, symbolized by the music of the flute, and yearns for total union with him.

Death of Kamsa

Preparations for a large festival were afoot in Mathura, and Kamsa, now fully aware of the existence of Krishna, instructed two of his best wrestlers to maul Krishna and Balarama once they arrived at the sporting events included in the festivities. Furthermore, the fierce elephant Kuvalayapida was armed with an iron bar at the entrance to the arena, ready to kill the two youths. Kamsa then despatched Akrura, a great devotee of Krishna, to fetch Nanda and the boys and take them to the capital under the pretext of paying the annual tribute and participating in the celebrations. The day of departure soon arrived and the milkmaids were stricken with immense grief at the prospect of Krishna's departure, bitterly remarking that once he became accustomed to the sophisticated ladies of Mathura he would forget them. The party arrived at Mathura and on reaching the arena Krishna saw the huge divine bow at the centre of the celebrations, guarded by armed men. He quickly picked it up, strung it, and it snapped in two with a tremendous noise. Kamsa was struck by panic and understood that Krishna and Balarama had arrived. The mad elephant Kuvalayapida, and shortly afterwards the wrestlers, were killed by the two brothers. Krishna then entered the arena, dashed onto the dais on which Kamsa was seated, hurled him to the ground and dragged him in the dust by his hair. The crowds rejoiced at the death of the tyrant. Krishna and Balarama then met their parents and took leave of Nanda, promising to visit him later.

Krishna, armed with an elephant tusk, grabs Kamsa by the hair and drags him from the throne. Folio from a Bhagavata Purana *manuscript. Opaque watercolour on paper, Basohli, Panjab Hills, c. 1725.*

Life in Mathura

However, events took another turn. The boys first underwent a series of rituals and were taught various subjects, including the use of different weapons in prospect of facing the formidable enemy, Kamsa's father-in-law, Jarasandha. He resented Kamsa's death and decided to avenge him by eliminating Krishna, Balarama and their clan, the Yadavas (descendants of Yadu). The long and bloody war took its toll on Mathura and the Yadavas, and soon another danger appeared: the barbarian Kalayavana and his troops invaded the land and laid siege to Mathura. With the mighty king killed, Krishna and Balarama decided to move the whole population from Mathura to Dwarka, on the west coast of India.

Krishna in Dwarka and his part in the Mahabharata War

The life and duties of a king occupied Krishna's life: he married some sixteen thousand princesses and participated in a number of political and military events, the most important being his part in the war between the Kauravas and their cousins, the Pandavas. This is the central theme of the *Mahabharata*. The five Pandavas were related to Krishna through Kunti, the mother of the three older brothers and sister of Vasudeva. Krishna was especially close to the hero Arjuna (white) and gave him his sister, Subhadra, in marriage. His role as an able counsellor is prominent in the negotiations between the rival factions. When all diplomatic efforts failed, both the Kauravas (descendants of Kuru) and the Pandavas (descendants of Pandu) sought his help. Krishna offered them the choice of his strong army, or himself alone and non-combatant. Arjuna chose the second option and Krishna acted as Arjuna's charioteer. When Arjuna lost heart seeing a number of relatives, friends, teachers and companions on the side of the Kauravas, Krishna delivered a famous sermon, known as the *Bhagavadgita* (the song of the Blessed One). In this he expounded the nature of action and inaction, the meaning of life, the transitory aspects of the individual and the various ways to attain God. At the crucial moment, Krishna revealed himself to Arjuna in his universal form. The vision became even more terrifying when Krishna revealed himself in the aspect of all-devouring Time. The war was long and fierce, many heroes died on both sides, yet eventually the Pandavas won. Krishna led them to pay their respects to the parents of the Kauravas, the old, blind king, Dhritarashtra, and his wife, Gandhari, whose hundred sons had lost their lives on the battlefield. While the king reconciled himself to his fate, the queen cursed Krishna to witness the destruction of his own clan, the Yadavas.

The end of the Yadavas and death of Krishna

A tragic series of events prompted the end of the Yadava clan. Some youths, one of whom was dressed as a woman, approached three sages asking them to predict the sex of the child 'she' was carrying. The sages, insulted by the arrogant behaviour of the young men, cursed them saying that 'she' would give birth to a club that would crush the Yadava race. The club was indeed born and was immediately crushed to dust and scattered, but particles of the iron dust turned to rushes which grew everywhere. One part of the club could not be crushed and was thrown into the sea; a fish swallowed it.

Meanwhile, the gods had requested that Krishna return to heaven, which he agreed to do since the destruction of the Yadavas had already begun. Seven days later, he urged the Yadavas to hasten to Prabhasa on a pilgrimage, and he and Balarama accompanied them. There the Yadavas performed all the customary rituals and, having bathed in the sea, they began to drink. A drunken brawl ensued and the Yadavas fell upon each other with their weapons. Their weapons expended, they resorted to the rushes, which became iron clubs in their hands. Krishna could not stop them and, eventually, not a single Yadava was alive; the only survivors were Krishna and Balarama. Krishna retired to the forest, where he noticed Balarama resting at the foot of a tree. From his mouth issued a huge snake, the mighty Ananta, who slithered towards the ocean. While Krishna sat lost in thought, a hunter called Jara (old age) approached. His arrow was tipped with the iron of the club recovered from the fish's stomach. Mistaking Krishna's foot for a deer, he shot at it. When he realized his mistake, he fell at the feet of the god, who calmly blessed him before dying. At that very moment the age of Kali began, and Dwarka disappeared in the waters of the sea, marking a great moment in time.

The myths presented here demonstrate the precariousness of creation, which is torn between good and evil. To re-establish a balance between these two polarities, the gods intervene; first and foremost is Vishnu in one of his many aspects. Here again, one of the crucial aspects of Hindu thought is the awareness of the impermanence of creation, which is poignantly expressed in the life-stories of Rama and Krishna. Even the gods, as all else, must die, only to re-appear in due course.

Destruction

The myth of the destruction of the sacrifice of Daksha (able, intelligent) sheds light on the difficult relationship between the followers of the orthodox Brahmanical establishment, exemplified by Daksha and the devotees of Shiva, the wild ascetic renowned for his unconventional religious practices. The enmity between Daksha and his son-in-law Shiva reaches a climax when Daksha's daughter, Sati (virtuous), is offended by her father's exclusion of her husband from an important religious ceremony and commits suicide. This episode unleashes Shiva's violence, personified by the god Virabhadra (auspicious hero). The following narrative is drawn from the *Shiva Purana*.

The gods and other divine beings were assembled at Prayaga (Allahabad) to celebrate a sacrifice when the great patriarch Daksha arrived. Every deity paid homage to him except his son-in-law, Shiva, who being the origin of the universe was exempt from such a duty. Daksha, however, was furious at this lack of respect and scathingly commented aloud on the incident, within the earshot of all.

Daksha himself then organized a solemn ceremony to which all were invited except his daughter Sati and her husband, Shiva, whom he now despised. By chance, Sati heard of the impending event and went to her father's house accompanied by a host of attendants. On her arrival, she entered her father's apartments 'like a flash of lightening' and criticized her father's behaviour in a dignified manner. Daksha, incensed by her remarks, heaped insults upon her and her husband and finally repudiated her, to which Sati retaliated by

Virabhadra. The striding four-armed god is flanked by the ram-headed Daksha (left) and by Sati (right). In his four hands he carries a bow and arrow, sword and shield. Engraved on either side of his head are a linga and a Nandi. Metal plaque, Karnataka or Maharashtra, eighteenth century.

A distraught Shiva carries the charred body of Sati on his shoulder. In the background Vishnu prepares to cut the body into pieces by throwing his discus. Coloured print, Bengal, first decade, twentieth century.

cursing Daksha. Sati then sat on the ground in silence, concentrating on Shiva, and such was the heat generated by her meditation that her body dissolved into mystic flames. At this, the assembled guests were struck with astonishment and horror. Her attendants, gathered at the door of Daksha's house, began to wail, some so grief-stricken they committed suicide, while others entered the sacrificial hall and attempted to disrupt the ceremony. A violent fight ensued and Sati's surviving attendants returned to Shiva and told him what had happened. Shiva plucked a lock of his matted hair and, in anger, threw it on a rock from which emerged the fear-inspiring Virabhadra (auspicious hero) and the awesome Mahakali (great Kali), both ablaze with anger. These two, accompanied by a host of ghosts and goblins, marched towards Daksha's house, where the ceremony had resumed after Sati's death. The course of the ritual was troubled by a number of bad omens which frightened both the gods and the other guests. Shortly after, Virabhadra and his hosts appeared in the sacrificial hall, but the efforts of the gods to prevent Virabhadra and his troops destroying Daksha's sacrifice were to no avail. A terrible battle ensued and eventually Virabhadra caught the terrified Daksha, who was trying to conceal himself, and threw him into the fire.

According to another version of the story, Shiva retrieved the charred body of Sati from the flames and carried it on his head as an act of penance. Fearing that Shiva's power would be greatly increased by this, Vishnu gradually cut Sati's body into pieces by throwing his discus, which lacerated her body. Each place on which the body parts fell became a 'seat of the goddess' and, in time, a pilgrimage site.

The burning of Kama

This episode, one of the most famous of Hindu mythology, has been a great source of inspiration for poets and artists. The youthful god of love, Kama (desire), is visualized as a handsome young man. He rides in a parrot-drawn chariot, armed with a sugarcane bow, with a string formed by a row of buzzing bees and five floral arrows which symbolize the five senses. He arrives on the scene accompanied by his wife Rati (lust) and his ally Vasanta (spring). The god of Spring, like an able stage-manager, provides all the necessary props: birds, flowers, trees, blossoming shrubs and perfumed breezes which ensure the success of Kama's mission. The following myths are drawn from the *Shiva Purana*.

At that time Parvati was devoutly looking after Shiva. She brought flowers daily to him, but he was absorbed in meditation and was unaware of her presence. It became imperative to distract the thoughts of the meditating god, and Indra sought the help of Kama, who was accompanied by his beloved wife, Rati, and Vasanta, the god of Spring. These three descended to earth, where Shiva was deep in thought. At that moment Vasanta transformed the forest where Shiva lived into a garden in full bloom, inhabited by warbling birds and humming bees. The soft breeze, redolent with the perfume of various trees, ravished the minds of the ascetics and awakened in them thoughts of love. Kama and Rati began to flirt near Shiva with the intent of deflecting his thoughts.

Parvati, accompanied by her maids, arrived with flowers for Shiva. Noticing that her presence had momentarily distracted Shiva, Kama shot at him with one of his lotus-tipped arrows and, at that moment, Shiva was made aware of her beauty. Although unsettled by this, Shiva immediately regained control of his thoughts and suspected the presence of Kama nearby. He spotted Kama concealed, aiming another arrow at him. Even before the gods assembled could ask for mercy, a tremendous fire emitting the light of myriad suns issued from Shiva's third eye and incinerated Kama. Parvati was greatly perturbed and, accompanied by her maids, she returned to her father's palace, while Kama's wife, Rati, beat her breast and plucked her hair in despair at her husband's fate. On seeing Rati's distress, the gods pleaded with Shiva on her behalf. He promised that Kama would eventually be reborn as the son of Krishna and Rukmini, and that a brilliant future was in store for him.

Parvati's penance

The aim of Parvati's penance was the conquest of Shiva. This example is one of many instances in which the fire of love and the fire of asceticism mingle. The theme of Parvati's penance is enduringly popular within Hindu mythology. Poets have delighted in the minute descriptions of the various penances, such as standing on one leg for hundreds of years and then on only one toe. The current version of the story is particularly detailed; the account of the visit by Shiva's emissaries to test Parvati's theological knowledge and faith is told at length. This is unsurprising within the context of a Shaiva text, written for the

The god Shiva marries Parvati, who is shown here being given away by her father.
Detail from a ceiling painting, Virupaksha temple, Hampi, Karnataka, late eighteenth to
early nineteenth century.

propagation of Shaiva faith. A particularly human moment appears in the description of Parvati's parents' perplexity and anxious concern when she reveals her resolve to marry the unconventional Shiva.

In the meantime, Parvati could not forget Shiva. She was deeply in love and could think of nothing else. One day, Narada, the great sage and divulger of all divine gossip, suggested she please Shiva by performing severe austerities. The opposition of her parents notwithstanding, Parvati embraced a life of asceticism. During the summer she performed the five fire penance, sitting motionless in the sun, surrounded by four flames. In the rainy season she let the rain drench her; in winter she stood immersed in the freezing water, concentrating all the time upon Shiva. For three thousand years this continued, during which time she constantly reduced her food intake and, by the end, she existed on air alone.

Throughout this, her father tried to dissuade her from continuing her penance, arguing that Shiva was nowhere to be seen, but Parvati remained steadfast in her resolve. The time came when the spiritual heat emanating from her person was such that it scorched the gods. They approached Shiva and, after singing his praises, explained the reason for their visit: Parvati's penance could only end if he married her. After lengthy discussion Shiva agreed to marry but, before doing so, he sent various sages to test her steadfastness. She replied at length to all their questions but Shiva, not fully convinced of her determination, decided to give her the ultimate test. He appeared to her in the form of a Brahmin, was critical of the Shaiva doctrine and examined her on several difficult philosophical topics. Eventually, he revealed himself to her in his true form, and in due course the marriage was celebrated in the presence of all the gods and celestial beings.

The birth of Kumara and the end of Taraka

Once the nuptials were duly celebrated, Shiva and Parvati retreated to their Himalayan abode and passed their time in amorous activities. This lasted for such a long time that the cosmic order began to erode. To the great dismay of the gods, there was no hint that Parvati had conceived the long-awaited son of Shiva who was destined to destroy Taraka (an anti-god whose severe penance generated an intense heat which threatened to destroy the cosmos). The story of the conception and birth of Karttikeya (also known as Kumara) follows. This, one of the most involved narratives of Hindu mythology, reveals the complex nature of one of the main gods of the Hindu pantheon. Shiva, Agni, the wives of the seven mythical seers (identified with the stars of the Great Dipper), a mountain and eventually the river goddess Ganga, all play a role. It is therefore unsurprising that the personality of Karttikeya is one of the most elusive and mysterious of Indian lore. The following narrative is drawn from the *Shiva Purana*.

The gods grew restless and sent Brahma and Vishnu to Shiva, to discuss the matter of the non-forthcoming offspring. Once at Shiva's mansion, Shiva opened the door and in so doing spilt some semen upon the ground. The fire god, Agni, swallowed it, but since the seed was burning he felt extreme discomfort. By chance, the wives of the seven sages were bathing in the river on a winter morning and, feeling the cold, six of them gathered around a fire to warm themselves, while the seventh, who suspected some foul play, warned the others and avoided the flame. Agni passed the fiery seed of Shiva to the six women warming themselves near the flame. Once the pregnancy of the six was known, they were repudiated by their husbands and forced to retreat into the forest. Later, unable to bear the fiery seed, they discarded it onto a mountain. The mountain, too, was scorched by the heat and hurled the seed into the

Ganga who, in turn, deposited it upon the grass. There, to the great joy of the gods, the semen transformed itself into a beautiful boy. In time, he was educated in the arts and sciences and given miraculous weapons, in preparation for the ensuing battle between himself and Taraka, whom he eventually defeated.

Shiva destroys the three aerial cities

One of the most famous episodes in Shaiva mythology is Shiva's destruction of the three aerial cities (*Tripura*) of the anti-gods, with a single shot. In this incident, Shiva faces a dilemma: the three sons of Taraka threaten the universe through the power of the merits they have acquired. On the other hand, they are great devotees of Shiva, which precludes any action on the part of the gods. By a daring strategy, the fall of Taraka's sons is engineered by Vishnu who, in connivance with Shiva, sends an heretical preacher, generally identified by commentators as a Jaina, to convert the anti-gods to the new creed, thereby abandoning the tenets of Shaivism. Thereafter Shiva, with the help of all the gods, semi-divine beings and celestials, is able to destroy the three cities. The following account is drawn from the *Shiva Purana*.

Taraka had three sons who, on the death of their father, decided to embrace a life of asceticism. They retreated into the forest and engaged in penance and meditation. After some thousand years of such a life, they were reduced to mere skin and bone. Brahma, pleased with their devotion, encouraged them to speak of their wishes. They asked to be forever young and be spared the miseries of sickness and death. Brahma explained that, being mortal himself, he could not bestow the gift of immortality upon them, so they should request an alternative. After much thought, they requested three cities, each stocked with all conceivable riches and other goods, and so well fortified that even the gods could not capture them. Furthermore, the cities should be mobile, enabling each of Taraka's sons to move around the earth and the sky. The eldest of the three requested a city of gold; the second, a city of silver and the third, a city of steel. Once every thousand years the three cities should meet and only Shiva, if ever so inclined, could destroy them with a single arrow. Clearly this was an impossibility since the three sons were great devotees of the Lord. Brahma complied with their wishes.

Immediately, Maya, the architect of the anti-gods, began to build the cities: one in the ether, one in the air and one on earth. They were furnished with all luxuries: temples, palaces, gardens, orchards, pools, and streets full of people plying different trades. When the work of the divine architect was completed, Taraka's sons took up residence.

Indra and the other gods were displeased with this arrangement because the three anti-gods were leading exemplary lives, engaging in meritorious activities and scrupulously following the tenets of the scriptures. In short, they were acquiring merit and power over the entire universe. Having considered the problem for some time, they approached Shiva, sang his praises and explained their plight, but Shiva replied that since the sons of Taraka were his devotees, he was unable to help and suggested they visit Vishnu. Vishnu instructed the distressed gods to worship both Shiva and the Lord of Sacrifices. While they

Shiva, mounted on his chariot, aims at the three converging cities of the anti-gods. Wooden panel of the ceremonial chariot of the Kumbeshvara temple, Kumbakonam, Tamil Nadu, twentieth century.

did so, thousands of goblins, fully armed, emerged from the sacrificial fire and, at the command of Vishnu, invaded the three cities of the anti-gods, only to be reduced to ash. Vishnu was greatly perplexed and devised another plan; the power of the anti-gods was based on their devotion to Shiva and the correct observance of the rituals so that only the disruption of their religious practices could undermine their ever-increasing might.

Through his powers of delusion, Vishnu then created a preacher, who visited the three cities and converted the anti-gods to a new doctrine. Thus they neglected the worship of Shiva and the teaching of the scriptures. They no longer bathed on auspicious occasions or bestowed gifts on religious institutions, the women stopped serving their husbands, and their husbands tried to seduce other men's wives, so that both religious and social orders were subverted. On seeing this, the gods approached Shiva again, who agreed his devotees had strayed from the path of virtue and consented to kill them.

To achieve this, a magical chariot and special arrow were fashioned for him. The chariot was made from gold, its right wheel was the sun and its left, the moon. Numerous deities presided over the spokes of the wheels and constellations embellished its sides. The various divisions of time formed the tip of the chariot, the axle-shaft, the bottom of the carriage and its poles. The *mantras* were its tinkling bells and the four *Vedas* were the horses which drew it.

Brahma was the charioteer, the Lord of Mountains became the bow and the Lord of Serpents acted as the string. Vishnu became the arrow, and Agni its fiery tip. In short, the entire universe was contained in the chariot. Shiva stood in readiness for thousands of years, waiting for the three cities to converge. At the auspicious moment, Shiva drew his bow and released an arrow of a brilliance comparable to that of countless suns. The arrow constituted by Vishnu and Agni burnt the three cities and their ash fell into the ocean.

The origin of Devi and the killing of Mahishasura

The immensely powerful Mahishasura (buffalo-*asura*) proves to be a threat to the gods. The force of their joint meditation creates an all-powerful female being, the Devi (goddess), also known as Durga, who eventually kills their antagonist. The following account is drawn from the *Shrimad Devi Bhagavatam*.

Through severe penance and steadfast meditation, Mahisha obtained from Brahma the favour which decreed he could not be killed by anyone except a woman. This granted, his pride swelled to such an extent that he regularly robbed the gods of their due share of oblations, insulting and harassing them in every possible way. Tired, frightened and in despondent mood, the gods decided to pool all their energies. A brilliant fire emanated from Brahma's face; an unbearable flame issued from Shiva's body, and a dazzling, blue light emerged from Vishnu. Similarly, variegated tongues of fire emerged from Indra, Agni, Kubera, Varuna and many more gods. This mass of fire and light merged in front of their very eyes and, to their amazement, a most beautiful goddess was born. Her face was fair, her eyes black, and the palms of her eighteen hands as well as the soles of her feet were copper-red. Each part of her body was generated by the energy of the various gods. As she emerged from the flame, the gods gave her presents: the Himalaya offered her various precious stones and the lion that became her conveyance, Vishnu gave her a discus, Shiva a trident, Varuna a conch and Indra a thunderbolt. When she was fully adorned and armed, the gods began to chant her praises and pleaded their cause. The goddess promised to fight against Mahisha immediately. The thought of the gods being intimidated by Mahisha amused her, and she laughed a long, hoarse laughter at which the earth trembled.

That roar and ensuing earthquake struck terror in the hearts of the anti-gods who, at the behest of Mahisha, sought the cause of such tremor. When they spied Devi, splendid in her clothes and jewels, drinking wine from a golden cup, they were struck with wonder and dared not speak to her, but immediately reported back to Mahisha. Excited by their glowing descriptions, Mahisha ascertained she was unmarried and sent his prime minister to her with a proposal of marriage. At the end of a long conversation during which the prime minister exhibited all his negotiating skills, Devi categorically refused the proposal.

Disappointed at the failure of the diplomatic mission, Mahisha summoned his ministers: one suggested the king should conquer her by force; another interpreted Devi's harsh words as a sign of passion and her violence simply a

Durga slays Mahisha. The ferocity of the attack is clearly expressed in the way the goddess forces back the neck of Mahisha and thrusts her trident into his throat. To the right, the lion mauls one of the victim's arms. Bhubaneshvar, Orissa, Vaital Deul temple, late eighth century.

disguise for her amorous feelings; a third felt that she was an aspect of *maya*, the divine illusion, and that her presence did not bode well for either Mahisha or his subjects.

Another messenger was sent to Devi in the hope of persuading her to accept Mahisha's proposal. Again she refused. Her anger caused earth tremors, fearful noises and frightened the anti-gods. Mahisha sent his most distinguished warriors to fight against her, but they were all defeated so he resolved to go himself to the battlefield. He discarded his buffalo body, assumed that of a handsome man and approached Devi with sweet words. Eventually, she told him she had been created to kill him and invited him to either flee to the netherworld or fight against her. Mahisha, however, took no heed of her words and continued courting her, until she reiterated his choice. Mahisha resolved to fight. It was a terrible battle, in which some of the most distinguished followers of Mahisha fell. Stunned by their death, he elected to fight Devi in person. Since arrows and spikes were not powerful enough, Mahisha resorted to magic tricks; transforming himself into a lion he clawed Devi's lion, then assumed the guise of an elephant and threw rocks at her. When attacked by Devi's lion, he became a mythical animal, the *sharabha,* and jumped on her. When Devi struck his head with her axe, he resumed his buffalo form and wounded her with his horns. He then caught hold of the mountains with his tail and hurled them at her. Eventually, after a fortifying drink of wine, Devi brandished her trident and pursued him. Finally, she spiked him on her trident and decapitated him with her discus, leaving the battlefield amid songs of praise from the gods and celestial beings.

Final dissolution

The following description of the final dissolution is drawn from the *Vishnu Purana* in which Vishnu assumes the form of Rudra, the destructive persona of Shiva, and proceeds to set the world ablaze. The seven main rays of the sun which are mentioned in this myth are, according to Hindu astronomy, the most important among its many thousands. These seven are all identified by name and supply heat and light to the moon, stars and the planets Mercury, Venus, Mars, Jupiter and Saturn. The blaze is followed by a flood and then a period of quiescence and regeneration.

At the close of one of Brahma's many life-spans, the earth is almost completely exhausted. A terrible period of famine follows, during which all beings die. Vishnu assumes the character of Rudra, the destroyer, and descends to reunite all his creatures with himself. After this he enters into the seven rays of the sun, drinks all the waters of the globe and all the moisture in living bodies so that the soil evaporates and dries the earth. The seas, rivers, mountain torrents and springs become exhausted, as do the waters of Patala in the subterranean regions. The seven solar rays, fed with abundant moisture, develop into seven suns whose radiance glows above, below, and on all sides, setting the three worlds and Patala on fire. Consumed by these suns, the three worlds become rugged and deformed. The earth, bare of verdure and devoid of moisture, resembles the shell of a tortoise. Hari (Vishnu), the destroyer of all things, becomes, in the form of Rudra, the scorching breath of the serpent Shesha which reduces Patala to ashes. When all the divisions of Patala have burnt, the great fire spreads to the earth and utterly consumes it. A vast whirlpool of eddying flame spreads to the atmosphere and the sphere of the gods, enveloping all in a blaze.

Having consumed the world, Vishnu, in the person of Rudra, breathes forth heavy clouds resembling vast elephants which overcast the sky, emitting roars and darting lightning. Some are as black as the blue lotus; some white as the water-lily; some dusky like smoke; some of a dun colour; some like ashes sprinkled on the forehead; some deep blue as the lapis-lazuli; some azure like sapphire; some as white as a conch or jasmine; some black as collyrium; some the bright red of a lady-bird; some coloured with the fierceness of red arsenic; some like the wing of the painted jay. Some are as large as towns or mountains, some as houses or hovels and some like columns. Both mighty in size and loud in thunder, they fill all space. Showering down torrents of water, these clouds quench the dreadful fires which envelop the three worlds. The rain lasts uninterrupted for a hundred years, flooding the whole world and pouring down in large drops, filling the middle region and inundating heaven. The world is enfolded in darkness and, though matter both animate and inanimate no longer exists, the clouds continue to pour down their waters.

When the universal spirit awakes, the world is revived; when his eyes close, all things fall upon the bed of mystic slumber. In like manner, as a thousand great ages constitute a day of Brahma, so his night spans an equal period, during which the world is submerged by a vast ocean. Awakening at the end of his night, the unborn Vishnu, in the character of Brahma, creates the universe anew.

Two principal themes dominate this chapter. Firstly, the constant threat posed by the anti-gods, and secondly, the force of fire. The gods are always in danger of dethronement from their rivals, whose power arises from their practise of asceticism. Thus the gods are forced to grant their enemies extraordinary favours. Nevertheless, the favours granted eventually prove to be the undoing of the anti-gods.

Fire appears in a variety of diverse aspects throughout this selection of myths, beginning with the fire of Daksha's ritual which symbolizes the preservation of the established law and order, and ending with the great conflagration, which eventually engulfs the entire universe.

Veiling and unveiling:
the divine power of delusion

Am">Among the five activities of the divine, the veiling of the ultimate reality through apparitions and the creation of delusion (*maya*) is the most elusive. The mystery of this divine power is explored in a number of myths. The seer Narada (the grand old man of Hindu mythology), or the equally renowned Markandeya, try in vain to pry through the veils of delusion and grasp its ultimate meaning. Although this faculty is common to all gods, the most famous myths centre upon Vishnu's *maya*. One of the many aspects of the Devi is Mahamaya or 'great delusion'. Through her divine power, she makes the universe appear as if it actually exists and thus is knowable by the senses. She is ever-present in creation, but manifests herself only to carry out some divine purpose. The following myth is drawn from the *Matsya Purana*.

The mystery of Vishnu's power of delusion

Kamadamana (queller of desires) was a young prince who, in accordance with his name, led a life of austerity. His father, concerned for his future, asked him why he would not marry and start a family. The youth remained silent out of respect for his father but, since his father insisted on an answer, he eventually replied that the all-encompassing Vishnu had revealed his divine power to him. The king pondered this, but reminded his son again of his duties to be married, to father children for the continuation of the family lineage and to perform the various religious obligations required.

The young man replied that he had already lived innumerable lives; he had experienced the miseries of birth and death hundreds of times. He had felt the pangs of love in union and separation. He had been a blade of grass, a shrub, a tree, a domestic and a wild animal, both man and woman, a goblin, a ghost, an attendant of the gods and a heavenly nymph. In short, there was no existence he had not experienced. Yet each time creation dissolved, he did likewise, only to be reabsorbed and born into another life when creation began anew. All of this happened because he had previously succumbed to the lure of delusion and had married.

To illustrate this, the young man told his father about his last but one incarnation. At that time, he was born as the recluse Sutapas (one whose asceticism is good). His steadfast devotion to Vishnu resulted in the appearance of the god on his divine eagle, Garuda, who promised to fulfil his most cherished wish.

Sutapas requested that Vishnu explain to him the secret of his power of delusion. Vishnu asked what he would do once he had understood and, instead, offered him a fulfilled life with sons, riches, pleasures and health. Sutapas argued that worldly pleasures were exactly that from which he sought freedom, but Vishnu objected, claiming no one had, or ever would, understand *maya*. He told Sutapas that a long time previously, Narada, the great seer, concentrated his thoughts on him for a long time and asked to be granted the favour of understanding the secret of *maya*. Although Vishnu tried to dissuade Narada from this course of action, the stubborn sage had insisted.

Vishnu had directed him to dive into a nearby lake, saying he would understand the essence of the divine power of delusion. Narada jumped into the water and emerged as a young girl, Sushila (the virtuous), daughter of the king of Varanasi.

When Sushila came of age, her father married her to the son of King Vidarbha. When the old King Vidarbha died, his son succeeded him. During all these years, Narada as Sushila enjoyed a fulfilled life. She had children and grandchildren, riches and health. Yet gradually a disagreement between her father and her husband degenerated into a fully-fledged war. In a single day, she lost her father, her husband, her children and grandchildren. Immediately she heard of this carnage, she rushed to the capital city and visited the battlefield, where she lamented the death of her family. She ordered a huge pyre to be erected and personally placed on it the bodies of her dead family. She lit the pyre and as soon as the flames began to rise she cried 'My son! My son!' Shortly afterwards, she jumped into the blaze. Suddenly, the fire became fresh and cool, the pyre became a lake, and Narada-Sushila found himself in the water again. Vishnu took him by the hand and asked who was the son whose death he was mourning. Narada remained silent and Vishnu explained he had experienced *maya*, the cursed power of delusion and the source of all sorrow. He continued by saying that nobody, not even the gods, could fathom this mystery, and his efforts to penetrate it were futile. In response, Narada requested that he be given the ability to remember the experience forever and to continue in his steadfast devotion to Vishnu. Furthermore, the waters of the lake should hold the power to erase sin and become a place of pilgrimage. Vishnu granted these wishes and disappeared.

Sutapas followed this story with rapt attention. Before leaving, Vishnu warned again that the secret of *maya* is unfathomable but, if he was still intent on trying, he could dive into a nearby lake and eventually he would learn the futility of his efforts. Sutapas dived into the water. Like Narada, he came out in the form of a young girl, and was fatally enmeshed in the net of a new existence.

The story of Madhu and Kaitabha

A recurrent theme in Hindu myths is that of *maya* as a magical divine power employed to confuse adversaries such as the mighty anti-gods Madhu and Kaithaba. The following myth is drawn from the *Srimad Devi Bhagavatam*.

Devi, called here Adi Shakti (primeval, feminine force), is presented as the personification of the power of delusion. In her forms of Yoganidra (yogic sleep), also known as Mahamaya (great delusion), she pervades Vishnu while he rests between one creative cycle and the next. As such, he is completely within her power and incapable of action until she withdraws from him. In this story she causes the downfall of Madhu and Kaitabha by granting the favour that causes their immeasurable pride and, eventually, their death.

Before the beginning of creation, while Vishnu was still asleep, some wax fell from his ear and from it emerged Madhu and Kaithaba. They played in the waters of dissolution for a long time until their inquisitive minds began to brood on the origin of the universe and other weighty questions, leading them to embrace a life of asceticism and meditation. After a thousand years, during which their thoughts had been fixed on the Great Goddess, she appeared before them and granted their request of invincibility and of choosing the moment of their death.

The two brothers returned to their pleasurable life in the water until they saw Brahma seated on the pericarp of the lotus issuing from Vishnu's navel. They began making fun of Brahma, saying he was an unfit hero for sitting on such a splendid lotus throne and that, if he was not a coward, he should come and fight with them. At this, Brahma became concerned and wondered what to do. He rapidly considered the four expedients of diplomacy: conciliation, bribery, sowing dissension and war, but decided none was adequate and the only solution to the impending problem was to awaken Vishnu. He concentrated his thoughts on the sleeping god and began to sing his praise; while chanting, however, he expressed his distress. After some time, Brahma, seeing that Vishnu was not arising from his sleep realized that only Adi Shakti, the supreme goddess who presided over Vishnu's slumber, could help. He fixed his mind upon her in her form of Yoganidra. At last, she condescended to leave Vishnu's body and, at the moment she did so, Vishnu slowly emerged from his sleep. Stretching and yawning, he asked Brahma why he was so perturbed, and on hearing the cause of Brahma's distress, reassured him that he would deal with the matter.

While Vishnu was speaking to Brahma, Madhu and Kaitabha appeared in the waters of dissolution. In their pride, they declared that either Brahma must agree to become their servant or they would kill him, and then Vishnu. When Vishnu heard this he challenged them to a fight. The two brothers advanced and proved to be invincible; once Madhu completed his round, Kaitabha began his, and, after some time, Vishnu tired. In the meantime, Adi Shakti and Brahma watched. Vishnu, exhausted, negotiated a truce, after which the battle would be resumed. While resting, Vishnu realized that Adi Shakti had granted the brothers the gift of dying when they chose, so he concentrated his mind on seeking her help in his plight. The goddess appeared in mid-air and encouraged Vishnu to recommence the fight, promising her assistance. Vishnu, Madhu and Kaitabha fought for a very long time, but Vishnu was again in distress. The goddess, laughing aloud, attracted the attention of the brothers. She fascinated them with her sidelong glances, her charms ravished their minds, and both fell madly in love with her. At that moment, Vishnu, who saw everything, condescended to admit defeat and requested them to ask for a boon from him, but they haughtily replied that it should be for Vishnu to ask for a gift from them. Vishnu requested to kill them both. The brothers were speechless. Seeing, however, that they were surrounded by water, they insisted on being killed on solid earth, with no water in sight. Immediately Vishnu's thigh expanded and became solid earth. Madhu and Kaitabha laid their heads upon it and Vishnu decapitated them with his discus.

The story of King Harishchandra

There are a number of myths in which the power of delusion is used to test the steadfastness of a human or deity. An important example is the story of King Harishchandra (having golden splendour), one of the most renowned kings of Hindu lore. He exemplifies rectitude and unflinching steadfastness and was reputedly a life-long example for Mahatma Gandhi. The following version of the myth is drawn from a Kannada work, the *Sri Pampa Mahatme*, probably compiled in the nineteenth century.

The story begins at the court of Indra, where the two rival ascetics Vasishtha and Vishvamitra meet and, as usual, fall into argument. Vasishtha declares Harishchandra to be the most truthful person in the universe, Vishvamitra disagrees, and sets his heart on demonstrating that Harischandra is not the faultless hero that Vasishtha proclaims him to be.

Leaf from a storyteller's book depicting the story of King Harishchandra. A shepherd flees from the wild beasts created by Vishvamitra that have invaded the countryside. Opaque watercolour on paper, Maharashtra (?), late nineteenth century.

Vishvamitra is invited by Harishchandra

Harishchandra celebrated an important fire sacrifice to which he invited all sages and ascetics. At its completion, the guests were rewarded with generous presents such as cattle, land and gold. Vishvamitra, one of the guests, received his share but, under some pretext, he entrusted it to the king saying he would collect it in due course.

Immediately Vishvamitra began to harass the king. Through his power of delusion he created pests and rodents to destroy the crops, scavenger birds to kill the smaller birds and animals, crocodiles to infest the rivers and ferocious monkeys to wreck the hermitages. As if all of this were not enough, a number of natural disasters such as floods, droughts, locusts and many others descended on Harishchandra's kingdom.

The distraught subjects reported this sad state of affairs to the king, who decided to eliminate the wild animals during a hunting expedition. Accompanied by Queen Chandramati and his son Rohitasva, the king visited the hermitage of the sage Vasishtha. The sage, aware of his rival's schemes, warned the king not to enter Vishvamitra's hermitage or the territory near it on any account.

The magical boar

On hearing of a royal hunt, Vishvamitra created a huge boar that ravaged the countryside. The terrified hunters asked the king for help. He in turn hit the boar with an arrow and the wounded animal ran through the forest towards the hills. The king, exhausted by the hunt, fell asleep to a series of ominous dreams. Among these were forecasts of the loss of both his kingdom and his status.

Suddenly, an excited group of hermits arrived at the royal camp claiming the king had pitched his tents on the grounds of Vishvamitra's hermitage, hence disrupting its quiet. The king was distraught at the prospect of having unwittingly disregarded the instructions of Vasishtha and resolved to visit the sage and beg for forgiveness. At this moment, the wounded boar appeared before Vishvamitra, who blessed it and turned his wrath towards the king. His anger was so deep that he started to perspire and in so doing created two beautiful girls who were accomplished in all the arts but, because they emerged from his drops of perspiration, they were untouchables. The sage blessed them and sent them to Harishchandra's camp to seduce him. They entered the presence of the king and charmed him with their music. In his enthusiasm, Harishchandra promised to reward them with whatever they wished. One requested the royal umbrella, but the king refused to part with the insignia of royalty. Then they asked to marry him and, again, the king refused because a *kshatriya* cannot marry two untouchables. A long discussion ensued and finally the irate king ordered the girls to be whipped and sent out of the camp. They returned to Vishvamitra's hermitage, while the king worried about these events and their possible consequences.

The king's disgrace

On hearing from the weeping girls all that had happened, Vishvamitra confronted Harishchandra regarding the trespassing of the boundaries of the hermitage. He told the king that his anger could only be placated by marriage to the girls. Harischandra replied that he was prepared to surrender his kingdom rather than marry two untouchables. Vishvamitra accepted and thus became the new ruler of Ayodhya. Having shown the kingdom to Vishvamitra, the royal family and the prime minister set off on their pilgrimage to Varanasi, but before taking leave of the king, Vishvamitra asked him to return the wealth that he had left with him at the time of the sacrifice. The king, by now deprived of his kingdom, had no money. Vishvamitra, furious, beat the queen in front of Harishchandra and insisted on being repaid. He sent his emissary, Nakshatraka, to remind the king that he had only one year to settle the debt.

Vishvamitra obstructs Harishchandra's pilgrimage

Through his power of delusion the ascetic made the progress of the king and his family extremely difficult. He created a dense forest in which they lost their way. At times the king thought he had lost either his wife, his son, the minister, or all three. He thought he was confronted by people blocking his way and by wild animals ready to attack him. Clouds gathered, and soon a thick rain and darkness engulfed the forest path. Suddenly, and from nowhere, Nakshatraka appeared and reminded him of his debt. Harishchandra assured him that he would pay his debt in one week's time upon arrival in Varanasi. A cyclone delayed the king's journey, followed by a scorching sun whose intense heat started a forest fire. The king, his family and the minister sought a way out from the blaze, but to no avail. The queen, ready to sacrifice herself, jumped into the flames, but awed by the force of her loyalty to her husband, the fire disappeared, leaving the queen untouched.

Harishchandra sells his wife, the queen

While on route to Varanasi, Nakshatraka again appeared, reminding the king of his debt to Vishvamitra. Harishchandra appeased him by saying the journey was almost complete and, on arrival in Varanasi, he would sell the queen, his son and himself to repay his debt to the sage. Hungry, thirsty and tired, they reached Varanasi and, no sooner had they arrived, than Nakshatraka reappeared clamouring for Vishvamitra's money. Harishchandra advertised the sale, and the queen encouraged him to sell her and their son first. They were bought by the Brahmin Kalakaushika. The deal concluded, Harishchandra handed over the money to Nakshatraka, but the debt had not been completely repaid. Nakshatraka reminded the king that he had only one day remaining to settle the matter. Harishchandra begged his minister to sell him but, to their great dismay, nobody was interested. At long last, Virabahu, an untouchable, bought the king.

Leaf from a storyteller's book depicting the story of King Harishchandra. Vishvamitra's emissary appears before Harischandra and his family bathing in the Ganges at Varanasi. Opaque watercolour on paper, Maharashtra (?), late nineteenth century.

Harishchandra works in the burning ground

On conclusion of the sale, Nakshatraka received the outstanding money and Harischandra began work in the household of Virabahu. The tasks of the king included sweeping, cleaning, looking after the animals and guarding the house. Such was the volume of work to be done that the king could not wash his own clothes and was too destitute to buy new ones. He was tired, hungry and despondent. Furthermore, Virabhahu's wife complained about him to her husband and Harischandra was moved to the burning ground, which was under the jurisdiction of Virabahu. There, among other tasks, he collected the money for cremations and undertook a number of menial jobs.

The fate of the queen did not much differ from that of the king. She was harassed by the wife of Kalakaushika, and by his sons, who were difficult and never pleased with her work. The prince, too, was employed in the Brahmin's household. Each day he went with other boys into the forest to collect wood, flowers and sacred grass for the Brahmin's rituals. One day, reaching for a tuft of grass near the hole of an anthill, he was bitten by a cobra and instantly the poison killed him. The other boys rushed back to tell his mother, but the queen was not allowed to leave the house until she had completed her work. At night, she managed to sneak to the forest where, despite the darkness, she found the body of her son.

The queen is sentenced to death

On finding her dead son, the distressed queen looked for a place to cremate the body. She saw the far-off flames of the cremation ground, but Vishvamitra decided to harass her further and created goblins, ghosts, ghouls and other terrifying visions to frighten her during her voyage. At the end of her strength and wits, the queen reached the cremation ground and put together a rudimentary pyre on which to place the body of her son. Suddenly, Harishchandra emerged from the darkness and smoke, heaping abuse on her for trespassing. Because she had not paid the tax for cremating her son's body he destroyed the pyre with a long stick. At this point, the exhausted queen revealed her identity, leaving Harishchandra transfixed to the spot while she carried away the body, concealed it in a safe place and returned to the house of the Brahmin in the hope of acquiring some money to pay the tax.

While on her way, she heard the screams of a young boy attacked by a gang of robbers and intervened, albeit too late. On hearing her, the robbers fled in great haste, dropping the stolen jewellery. Suddenly, the police arrived and despite her protests to the contrary, the queen was arrested and charged with murdering the boy. She was dragged before the King of Varanasi who, without even interrogating her, sentenced her to death. She was then taken to the very cremation ground where Harishchandra was working. Virabahu, in charge of both cremations and executions, ordered Harishchandra to decapitate her. While waiting to receive the fatal blow she cried 'May truth prevail!' and instead of cutting her neck, the sword bent itself around her like a floral wreath.

At this sight, Harishchandra was extremely perplexed. Vishvamitra and his retinue appeared before him. The sage recognized his exceptional truthfulness and burst out in great praise of his steadfastness. Shiva and the other gods gathered around the king and the queen, who in turn, worshipped them. The prince was revived and the family were carried in triumph through Varanasi, eventually returning to Ayodhya.

Within Hindu mythology the gods act not just from necessity but also from a sense of innate playfulness. This creates, sustains and destroys the universe, and also motivates their involvement in human affairs.

However, though the gods are involved in worldly matters, they maintain a sublime detachment for they know that this dazzling creation is nothing but a bubble, a figment of delusion. Mankind, however, is unaware of this, and believes this world permanent and worthy of attachment.

Maya has a further meaning. It designates the faculty to create and destroy, as exemplified in some of the myths narrated here. The gods are 'magicians, jugglers' and their creations are as ephemeral as acts of magic. The seekers, in the quest for release from worldly entanglements, will eventually realize this splendid act of magic as a creation of divine play and, ultimately, as nothing more than a tool of the gods.

Anugraha, the bestowal of grace

Aconsiderable number of myths centre on the benevolent aspect of the deities and on their ability to bestow grace on their devotees, be they animals, humans, anti-gods, demons or fellow gods. Most of the stories concentrate on devotion to a particular god with meditation, asceticism and selfless devotion (*bhakti*) as the means of achieving a set goal.

The descent of the Ganga

The background of the myth narrating the descent of the heavenly river Ganga (Ganges) to earth is a complicated story involving the ancestors of King Bhagiratha – the sixty-thousand sons of Sagara – who are burnt to ashes by the wrath of an ascetic. As part of the last rites Bhagiratha must immerse their remains in the waters of the holy river to ensure the smooth passage of their souls to the world of the ancestors. The following narrative is drawn from the *Ramayana*.

Bhagiratha was without issue and in the hope of remedying this problem he performed great austerities at Gokarna. Eventually, Brahma, pleased with his devotion, appeared and asked him to express his wishes. The king replied that his greatest desire was to offer the funerary libations to his ancestors. As part of the last rites the ashes had to be moistened by the water of the Ganga. Bhagiratha's second wish was for a son to continue his lineage. Brahma prophesied that a son would be born to the king in due course. Furthermore, since the earth would not be strong enough to withstand the impact caused by the fall of the heavenly Ganga, Shiva himself would be charged with checking the progress of her descent.

Bhagiratha then resumed his penance and worship of Shiva. After one year, the pleased god appeared and promised the king that he would carry the Ganga on his head. The river plunged down from the sky with great force, landing on Shiva's head, but lost her way, meandering amidst his matted hair. For some years she wandered among Shiva's locks. Eventually he let her flow into the lake Bindu. It was a magnificent sight to see her flowing down from the sky, with all the gods and celestial beings gathered to witness the exceptional event. Her waters were filled with quantities of crocodiles, fish, all sorts of aquatic creatures, and swarms of geese which accompanied her on her way to earth. Through its contact with Shiva's body, the water became endowed with the property of washing away sins. Everyone rejoiced, hosts of people bathed in the river and, refreshed, they followed her progress. Bhagiratha led the way in his royal chariot and the Ganga followed in his tracks. At last they arrived on the

Shiva in heroic pose prepares to receive the goddess Ganga who descends from the sky. This image is inspired by a famous work by the painter Raja Ravi Varma (1848–1906), renowned for his theatrical compositions inspired by classical myths and legends. Calendar print for the year 1914.

shore of the ocean and entered into the huge hole previously dug by the sons of Sagara. As soon as their ashes came into contact with the water they ascended to the world of the gods. Since her presence on earth, the Ganga is known as Bhagirathi, the daughter of King Bhagiratha. Shiva, who carried the goddess on his head, became known as Gangadhara (the carrier of the Ganga).

Arjuna and the hunter

One of the most famous episodes of the great epic *Mahabharata* concerns the hero Arjuna, one of the five Pandava princes. Arjuna is told that only the *pashupata*, a magical weapon belonging to Shiva, will enable him to win the battle against his cousins and rivals, the Kauravas. The story of Arjuna's penance, his dramatic encounter with a wild hunter (who is revealed to be Shiva in disguise), and the receipt of the magical *pashupata* weapon from the god is a theme which has been explored innumerable times in the Sanskrit and other literatures of India. The following narrative is drawn from the seventeenth-century Kannada poem called the *Shabarashankaravilasa*, by Shadaksharadeva.

Arjuna was in the forest engaging in severe penance to obtain from Shiva the *pashupata* weapon necessary to destroy the Kaurava forces. One day, Indra, in the guise of a human, passed by and taunted him, saying he had seen a great number of ascetics, but none carrying in one hand a rosary of beads and in the other a bow and arrow. Arjuna, however, was not distracted by Indra's sceptical remarks; on the contrary, he replied that his aim was to please Shiva by all possible means so as to acquire the *pashupata* weapon. Indra, who was in fact Arjuna's father, revealed himself in his divine form and blessed him.

The penance of Arjuna gained momentum. He started by taking a small quantity of food every third day in the first month, then every sixth day in the second, and by the fifth month he was living only on air. The heat of his asceticism made him incandescent and, because of it, the water of the sea boiled, the moon darkened and the sages, concerned by such intense penance, approached Shiva. They requested that a new forest be created, where they could practise their austerities undisturbed by Arjuna. Shiva assured them that he would solve their problem by granting Arjuna's wish.

Shortly afterwards, Shiva, Parvati and their hosts attired themselves as hunters and descended to Indrakila for a hunting spree. Suddenly, at the order of Shiva, Muka the anti-god appeared as a huge wild boar; just at the moment in which it rushed towards Arjuna it was hit by arrows, both from Shiva in his form as hunter, and from Arjuna. A discussion ensued between Arjuna and the hunter as to whom the prey belonged. The hunter criticized Arjuna for carrying the bow and arrows of a warrior while being an ascetic. Arjuna lost his temper and a fierce fight ensued. He showered a rain of arrows on the hunter who, unperturbed, caught all of them in flight. Then Arjuna hit him with his bow, but the hunter simply took it from him. Eventually the two decided to settle the matter with a boxing match. Arjuna defended himself with great skill and bravery and almost overpowered the hunter, but suddenly he received a violent blow and blood oozed from his nose and mouth. He then realized that his daily worship of Shiva must have been faulty and therefore the reason he was losing against the hunter. In no time, with some sand and mud, he prepared a *linga*, circumambulated it and, in the course of his prayers, decorated it with flowers. When he raised his eyes, he was amazed to see the head of the hunter decorated with the very same flowers. Perplexed, he offered more flowers to the *linga*, and again, the flowers appeared on the hunter's head. Arjuna then realized his adversary was Shiva himself. At this, he surrendered to him, throwing himself at his feet. Pleased with his steadfastness and determination, Shiva bestowed on him the *pashupata* while Parvati presented him with a second magical weapon. Then the divine couple and their followers retired to Mount Kailasa while Arjuna returned to his wife and brothers, ready to fight the Kauravas.

Vishnu and Prahlada

Although Prahlada (happiness) was born into a family of anti-gods, with many early myths alluding to his exploits against various deities, devotional Vaishnava literature has also characterized him as the epitome of the perfect devotee. His faith in Vishnu is so complete that he emerges unscathed from a number of horrific ordeals. Finally, the god himself descends in his form as Narasimha 'man-lion' to free him from his father's persecution. The following narrative is drawn from the *Vishnu Purana* and the *Bhagavata Purana*.

Hiranyakashipu (golden-robed) was an anti-god who had conquered the three worlds. Thus the gods were deprived of their powers and became his servants. He had also received a boon from Brahma stating he would not be killed by either a human or a god, neither inside or outside a building, and neither by day or by night. Proud of his power, Hiranyakashipu claimed the offerings made to the gods and eventually usurped Indra's throne.

Hiranyakashipu had a pious son, Prahlada, who was a fervent devotee of Vishnu. The boy was living in the house of his guru, where he was educated. One day, while visiting his father, he maintained that Vishnu was the highest among the gods. This deeply offended Hiranyakashipu, who was filled with pride at the thought of being the ruler of the universe. Incensed by his son's lack of respect for him, rather than at his devotion to Vishnu, he sent Prahlada back to his guru, heaping all kinds of abuse on him.

After a long time, father and son met again and Prahlada reiterated his unswerving faith in Vishnu. This was too much for Hiranyakashipu, who had hoped for a change of mind in his son. Filled with rage, he ordered his attendants to kill him. Prahlada was beaten, hurled into a pit filled with poisonous snakes, trampled upon by huge elephants, thrown into the fire, fed poisonous food and subjected to all possible tortures. He emerged unscathed from all of these ordeals, drawing strength from concentrating his thoughts on Vishnu.

Thereafter, the king summoned Prahlada into his presence and, desiring to test again his faith in Vishnu, he told him that if Vishnu was indeed the 'All-Pervading' as his son maintained, he should also be in a pillar. While saying this he was filled with scorn and kicked a pillar in the verandah. The pillar split in two and before him stood the terrible figure of Narasimha, the 'man-lion', with

The twelve-armed Narasimha disembowels Hiranyakashipu. The victim's entrails hang from the upper two hands of the deity. Prahlada is shown standing in respectful attitude to the left. Deities and other celestials scatter flowers on the victorious god. Opaque watercolour on paper, Thanjavur (?), Tamil Nadu, c. 1830.

his eyes fierce like molten gold and his majestic face surrounded by a bristling mane. He had terrible tusks and a tongue sharp as a razor blade which waved like a sword. His frowning eyebrows inspired terror, his ears were erect and motionless, his mouth and nostrils deep and dark like caves in a mountain, and his open jaws awe-inspiring. He had a towering stature, a short, powerful neck, a broad chest and slender waist. He was covered with hair as white as moon rays and was endowed with hundreds of hands. He grabbed Hiranyakashipu, laid him on his lap, and disembowelled him with his sharp claws. Since Narasimha was neither man nor animal and the killing took place on a verandah at dusk, the conditions laid down by Hiranyakashipu were respected.

Shaiva saints

The story of Kannappa Nayanmar

Kalahasti, an important pilgrimage centre in Andhra Pradesh, provided the backdrop for one of the many acts of grace by Shiva. This legend celebrates the extreme devotion of a Shaiva devotee, Kannappa, one of the sixty-three Shaiva saints or 'chieftains' (*nayanmars*) popular in Southern Indian tradition. The life story of Kannappa is narrated in Sekkilar's *Periya Puranam* (big *purana*), a twelfth-century text in Tamil containing the narratives of the lives of all the Shaiva saints.

Tinnappa, as Kannappa was known before being re-named by Shiva, was a hunter by profession. As a great devotee of Shiva, he used to offer the flesh of the animals he had killed to the *linga*. In order to test his devotion Shiva caused some water to ooze from the eye of the *linga* which Tinnappa was worshipping. The hunter, fearing that someone may have harmed the Lord's symbol, decided to remove one of his own eyes with which to replace the ailing one. As soon as the new eye was in place the water stopped flowing. After some time, Tinnappa noticed that the second eye of the *linga* was affected. Without hesitation, he proceeded to tear out his other eye to offer it, and since removing his second eye would have left him blind, he marked with his foot the spot where his second eye would be placed. As he was beginning to gouge out his eye, Shiva appeared, restored his eyesight and changed his name to Kannappa 'the one who gave his eyes to the Lord'. Pleased with his devotion, the god established that Kannappa should be near the *linga* forever. It is for this reason that an image of the saint is placed near the *linga*, and worship is offered first to Kannappa and then to the *linga*.

The story of Karaikkal Ammaiyar

Karaikkal Ammaiyar, whose name means 'the venerable mother from Karaikkal', is one of the few women-saints among the 'chieftains' as well as a great figure of early Tamil literature. She probably lived in the sixth century AD. Born in Karaikkal, a small town in Tamil Nadu located on the coast of the Bay of Bengal, she was from childhood a great devotee of Shiva. An account of her life is given in Sekkilar's *Periya Puranam*.

Punitavati was her real name. She was married very early in life to a merchant from Nagapattinam, Paramadatta. One day her husband sent home two mangoes for lunch, but before his return, an aged mendicant came by begging for food and Punitavati gave him one of the mangoes. At lunch Paramadatta ate the remaining mango and, since he enjoyed it enormously, he asked for the

The skeletal poetess is portrayed playing the cymbals while singing the praises of Shiva. The small fangs at the corners of her mouth indicate her fierce nature. Bronze, South India, eighteenth–nineteenth century.

second. Punitavati invoked Shiva's help and instantly a mango materialized in her hand. As Paramadatta tasted the mango, he immediately realized that its quality was far superior to that of the mangoes he had sent home. Later, Punitavati told him of the mendicant's visit and, at the behest of her husband to demonstrate what had taken place earlier, she requested a third mango from Shiva. The mango appeared in her hand but vanished at the very moment Paramadatta tried to reach for it. Deeply unsettled by his wife's extraordinary powers, Paramadatta left Karaikkal and sailed to a distant country where he greatly prospered. On his return, he settled in another town, married a second time and had a daughter. After a long search, Punitavati's relatives located Paramadatta's whereabouts and requested him to return. He did so only to declare that Punitavati was not his wife, but a goddess worthy of worship. On hearing this, Punitavati begged Shiva to free her forever from the burden of beauty and requested he grant her the grace of forever witnessing his dance. Her prayers were answered and, instead of the beautiful Punitavati, there stood a skeletal figure with sagging breasts, protruding fangs, prominent veins and tendons, all in all a true goblin, like those who accompany Shiva. From then on, the saint, who signed her forceful and gory verses 'Karaikkal *pey*', the 'Goblin from Karaikkal', took residence in Alangadu, where she spent the rest of her life singing the praise of Shiva.

Her image is often found sculpted or painted among the followers of Shiva who watch his cosmic dance, and a small temple is dedicated to her at Karaikkal.

Temple myths

Sri Nataraja temple, Chidambaram

Chidambaram, in Tamil Nadu, is one of the most sacred places of Shaivism. It is the place where Shiva performed the *ananda-tandava* or 'dance of bliss', one of his six cosmic dances (*tandavas*). The *ananda-tandava* symbolizes the five activities of Shiva: creation, maintenance, destruction, veiling and unveiling, and the bestowal of grace. A legend narrated in the *Chidambaram mahatmya* reveals the origin of the 'dance of bliss'. The famous image of Shiva as Nataraja (p.14) dancing in a ring of flames was inspired by this myth.

A number of 'heretical' sages lived in a pine forest and practised austerities and rituals which lacked both conviction and genuine devotion to Shiva. The god decided to teach them a lesson. He descended to earth in the guise of a handsome young ascetic and ordered Vishnu to transform himself into Mohini (the enchantress), a beautiful courtesan. Both began the expedition with a view to creating confusion among the ascetics. While Vishnu-Mohini seduced the sages one by one, Shiva did the same with their wives. Eventually the two gods and their followers met in the depths of the forest. The sages were shocked to see their naked wives sporting amorously with the young ascetic. They ultimately discovered the identity of the two seducers and were filled with shame and hatred against Shiva as the instigator of the daring plot, and so resolved to kill him.

Through their magical powers they organized a solemn ritual. From the sacrificial flame there emerged first a huge tiger which leapt on Shiva, but it was killed before it could harm him. Shiva then skinned it with the nail of his little finger and donned its skin. Secondly, the sacrificial flame yielded a magical trident. It flew towards Shiva, who caught it mid-air and held it in his right hand. Following this, a furious antelope rushed against him in an attempt to gore him, but was caught tightly in Shiva's left hand. Thus the baffled sages created a number of snakes but these, too, were taken by the god and draped upon his hair and person as ornaments. Hordes of demons followed, but Shiva ordered them to become his servants. A horribly grinning skull jumped out of the fire pit and Shiva placed it into his matted hair as if it were a crown. The sages made a drum, the hourglass-shaped *damaru*, and hurled it with a deafening sound against the god. Needless to say, this too was caught by him and held firmly in one hand. Finally, they created a deformed dwarf, Apasmara, the 'man without memory', who embodied ignorance and evil, and with him came a scorching flame. Shiva caught the fire in his hand and stepped on the back of the dwarf, breaking his neck, and danced the dance of bliss which made the universe tremble. At the end of the dance the converted sages fell at his feet. Shiva left the forest to return to his Himalayan retreat. However, at the request of a number of devotees who had practised severe austerities to be granted the privilege of witnessing the dance, Shiva forever dances his 'dance of bliss' in the golden hall at the heart of the Chidambaram temple.

The myth of Palani

Palani is one of the six important temples in Tamil Nadu connected with the career of the god Murugan (youth) who is also known as Shiva's son, Karttikeya. This myth attempts to link the physical features of the site with the shoulder-pole (*kavadi*) which pilgrims carry up the mountain. The myth is recorded in the Palani *sthalapurana*.

The famous seer Agastya was presented by Shiva with two hills, Shivagiri and Shaktigiri, which were to be used as a place of worship. Agastya was granted permission to transport them to Southern India. One day he met Itumban,

The devotee Itumban is shown on his long journey carrying two huge piles of rocks tied to a yoke, symbolizing the two mountains donated by Shiva to Agastya. Painting on cloth pasted on wood, Thanjavur, nineteenth century.

the demon who had survived the victorious campaign of Murugan against his chief, Sura, and his hordes. However, since Murugan's slaying of them, they lost their demonic nature and were able to reach heaven. In order to help them on their way, Itumban spent his time on earth praying for their welfare and performing the appropriate rites. Agastya was impressed by Itumban's good and pious nature and sent him to collect the hills.

When Itumban arrived to fetch the hills, a shoulder pole materialized from nowhere, and the eight great serpents who support the world became ropes to tie the hills to the pole. Thus laden, he began his journey southwards. Near Palani, however, he felt that his strength was ebbing and he put the hills down in order to rest. Once refreshed, he moved to resume his journey but, despite his best efforts to lift the hills, they could not be moved. Filled with amazement and disbelief, he climbed one of the hills and found a child playing under a tree. Itumban tried to chase him away, letting him know that he was a demon. The unperturbed child told him the hill was his home and that if Itumban wanted it, he should simply pick it up. At this Itumban jumped at the boy, who was in fact Murugan playing one of his tricks, and was effortlessly killed by him. When Itumban's wife heard of her husband's death, she implored Murugan to restore him to life, which he did. Once Agastya arrived there to worship Murugan, he ordered Itumban to remain and serve Murugan in order to attain salvation. The image of Itumban carrying the two hills tied to a yoke is a familiar sight in shrines dedicated to Murugan.

Animal devotees

A number of local legends focus on the theme of the animal devotee. According to the myths, temples were built on the spot where an animal had discovered and worshipped a divine being. Cows, elephants, peacocks, cats, mice, lizards, spiders, snakes and others are all celebrated as exemplary devotees. Most of these myths relate to temples in Southern India.

A spider, a snake and an elephant worship the Linga

The locale of this legend is again Kalahasti. The focus of devotion at Kalahasti is the great temple dedicated to Shiva in his form as Kalahastishvara 'Lord of Kalahasti'. The following story is narrated to pilgrims who visit the site.

A spider, snake and elephant worshipped Shiva, each with their own method. The spider spun a fine web above the *linga*, the snake placed a gem upon it and the elephant washed it with water. The snake, however, was unaware of the other two devotees. One day, approaching the *linga* to perform its daily devotions, it noticed some holy *bilva* leaves around it and some water. Thinking that someone was trying to defile the symbol of the Lord, it coiled around the *linga*, to discover the culprit. The next morning, the elephant came with water in its trunk and prepared to lustrate the *linga*, as was his habit. The snake, thinking that the elephant was defiling the *linga*, slithered into its trunk. At that, the elephant dashed its trunk against the *linga*, thereby crushing both the spider and the snake. Unable to bear the excruciating pain, the elephant died on the spot. Pleased with their devotion, Shiva released the three animals

Vishnu riding on Garuda saves the King of the Elephants. Note the god's discus stuck in the crocodile's neck. Coloured print on paper, early 1970s.

from the chain of birth and rebirth. Today pilgrims are shown some discolouration on the pedestal of the *linga*, which bears witness to the event.

The story of Gajendra

Vishnu, in his aspect of Karivarada (bestower of grace on the elephant) or simply Varadaraja (lord of grace), is worshipped in a number of shrines. The most famous is the Varadaraja temple at Kanchipuram, one of the three major Shri Vaishnava temples in Southern India. The story is given in great detail in the *Bhagavata Purana*.

Gajendra (King among the Elephants) and his wives were sporting in the paradise-like garden at the feet of the mythical mountain Trikuta, whose three peaks were made of gold, silver and copper. Feeling hot and thirsty, the king of the elephants decided to descend into a nearby lake to bathe and assuage his thirst. As soon as he stepped into the water, a crocodile caught one of his legs and, despite desperate efforts, Gajendra was unable to free himself from the monster's fangs. The struggle continued for a long time until finally, on the verge of drowning, Gajendra plucked a lotus flower with his trunk and, lifting it towards the sky, began to sing the praises of Vishnu. Pleased by the hymns, Vishnu appeared, riding upon the shoulder of the eagle Garuda, and saved Gajendra by killing the crocodile with his discus. Instantly, Gajendra, who originally was a king cursed to assume the shape of an elephant for not having shown due respect to Agastya, resumed his human form while the crocodile, who was originally a divine musician (*gandharva*) also cursed by a sage, returned to his semi-divine form.

This selection of myths illustrates the power of devotion, penance and steadfastness. The devotees have to endure tests, like Arjuna who must fight against Shiva in disguise before his adversary reveals his divine nature. The youth, Prahlada, suffers numerous tortures but remains steadfast in his devotion to Vishnu, who frees him from the persecutions of Hiranyakashipu by appearing as a man-lion.

A number of myths are connected to specific temples, where both human and animal devotees obtain the grace of Shiva after suffering self-mutilation or death. In the Chidambaram myth, Shiva and Vishnu unite to humiliate the hypocritical seers living in the pine forest, and finally Shiva dances his 'dance of bliss' for the benefit of his devotees. The myths of Palani and the story of the King of the Elephants show how death at the hands of a god leads to inclusion in the fold of the followers and, in the case of the crocodile, to a release from the curse and reversion to one's former nature.

Living legacy

I ndia is a country steeped in myth and filled with landmarks associated with its legendary past. There is no mountain, river, cave or landscape feature which is not connected with some deity: Mount Kailasa is regarded as the Himalayan abode of Shiva and the backdrop for numerous mythical events; Mount Govardhana near Mathura is the scene of many episodes of Krishna's life, and, of course, the most revered of all rivers is the Ganges, the goddess Ganga. Equal in sanctity with the Ganges is the Kaveri, celebrated as the Ganges of Southern India, along whose course are some of the most important temples and temple towns. Although officially only seven rivers are deemed sacred, in fact, every Indian river is regarded as sacred.

Not only mountains and rivers are linked to momentous mythical events. According to a well-known legend, Kerala emerged from the sea through the intervention of Parashurama, the sixth incarnation of Vishnu. Having exterminated the warrior class (*kshatriyas*), he searched for a place on uncontaminated ground where Brahmins could live in peace and dedicate themselves to the study of the scriptures and the celebration of rituals. Soon after, he arrived on the shore of the Arabian Sea. He threw his axe across the sea from Gokarna to Kanyakumari (Cape Comorin) and the thin strip of land that emerged as the result became known as Kerala.

The subcontinent is bound together by a complex network of holy places. Thus there are the four 'abodes of light' (*dhamas*) at the four cardinal points: Badrinath in the north, Puri in the east, Ramesvaram in the south and Dwarka in the west. In the south are the six holy places connected with the defining episodes in the life of Murugan. Scattered throughout the country are the twelve '*lingas* of light' (*jyotirlingas*), the one hundred and eight sacred sites of Vishnu. The list could be continued. In each there is at least one temple, shrine, bathing pool and landscape feature connected to a specific mythological incident. The climax of sanctity, however, is achieved in the town of Varanasi, where the energy of all the holy places of the country is combined.

Pilgrimage

Hindu religion emphasizes the importance of pilgrimage as a means of acquiring spiritual merit by visiting temples or sites in which the divine power manifests itself. With the rapid improvement of living conditions, the rise of a middle class and the ever-increasing transport possibilities, pilgrimages have gained momentum. It is now relatively easy to reach remote places which once were only accessible on foot, often after long treks on paths through rugged terrain.

The 'new goddess' Santoshi Mata, (Mother of Contentment), is shown here surrounded by her devotees participating in a fire oblation. An auspicious vase is prominently displayed with a coconut and mango leaves stuck in the spout. Coloured print on paper, c. 1995.

This increase in visitor numbers goes hand in hand with the expansion of the tourist trade, better facilities at pilgrimage places and a flourishing of art and literature focusing on the specific pilgrimage sites. The compilation of works narrating the foundation myths of temples (*sthalapuranas*) of only local importance, and the spiritual merit acquired from a visit to the area, has been greatly encouraged by the influx of people in recent years. The local *sthalapurana* is printed in English, Hindi and the regional Indian languages by a local press. Images of the local deities and their mythology are on sale and the temple attendants offer guided tours of the site, as well as encouraging donations for charitable causes.

New times, new deities

The old myths and legends are not forgotten but evolve to incorporate new characters. The unique elasticity of the Hindu pantheon allows for the creation of new deities such as Santoshi Mata (the Mother of Contentment) who emerged in the mid 1950s. These new figures are effortlessly incorporated into the families of either Shiva or Vishnu. In keeping with the traditional, cyclical concept of time, gods who were once 'out of fashion' are rediscovered, while others who were popular in the past no longer play a

The tutelary goddess of Madurai, Minakshi, stands on a lotus at the centre of the temple tank. A temple tower is in the background. The foreground shows a view of the temple and the city. Coloured print on paper, early 1970s.

prominent role. Regional gods can suddenly become relevant outside their traditional terrain. One of the most spectacular examples is that of Ayyappan, traditionally a god worshipped only in a very circumscribed region in the hilly area on the border between Tamil Nadu and Kerala. In the last forty years or so, Ayyappan has become a major south Indian god. Pilgrims flock from as far afield as Maharashtra, Andhra and Karnataka to his temple at Sabarimalai, which is only open for a limited period during the winter months. The last part of the journey, which must be covered barefoot, entails a long and difficult path through a forest before reaching the shrine itself.

Popular art

The importance of the legendary heritage is best seen in the prolific output of popular religious art, which strikes even the most casual observer of the Indian street scene. Every visitor to India is familiar with the ubiquitous and vibrant 'calendar prints' which represent gods, goddesses, mythical events and recently even movie stars. This variegated multitude stares at the passers-by from pavement displays, walls of public offices and homes. Images of gods, goddesses and saints are available not only as prints, but also as metal buttons provided with magnets which can be placed on the dashboard of the car or on the refrigerator door at home. In the last decade, three-dimensional plastic images have replaced the older versions which were made from china or plaster of Paris. The current fashion is to produce them complete with miniature temples enlivened by garlands of little red and green light bulbs which flash at regular intervals.

It is interesting to note that in the last fifty years or so, politicians such as Mahatma Gandhi, Pandit Nehru, Dr Ambedkar and more recently Mrs Indira Gandhi have reached an almost divine status and have themselves been incorporated into the repertoire of 'calendar prints'. Their lives are slowly entering the realm of myth. One of the most striking examples is a painted scroll from Bengal representing the life of Mrs Gandhi. In its last scene, the assassinated Mrs Gandhi is depicted ascending to heaven, welcomed by all the gods, sages and divine beings. This is no surprise since during her lifetime Mrs Gandhi saw herself, and was perceived as, a form of Durga, the slayer of the anti-god Mahisha.

Deities are also found in the most unlikely of scenarios (from a Western point of view). Thus, a leading brand of snuff has the six-headed god Karttikeya on its packets, the elephant-headed Ganesha advertises a famous brand of local cigarettes. Numerous deities are displayed on stickers on bales of cloth, incense sticks and fireworks, and many other products carry the image or name of particular gods or goddesses.

Film and TV productions

Modern technology has been a useful tool in popularizing mythology and legend. The Indian film industry began in 1912 with films such as R.G. Torney's *Pundalik*, inspired by the life of a Marathi Vaishnava saint. This was followed in rapid succession by a film based upon selected episodes from the *Ramayana*, and a year later by D.G. Phalke's *Raja Harishchandra*, an epoch-making production which laid the foundation of the biggest film industry in the world. Mythological films proved a box office success, and even the actors appearing in them were perceived (in the popular imagination) as an emanation of the deity they portrayed.

The most important example of the reciprocal relationship between myth and film is demonstrated in the film *Jai Santoshi Ma* (1975) which practically launched, single-handed, the cult of Santoshi Mata, mentioned above.

More ambitious projects such as the television versions of the *Ramayana* and that of the *Mahabharata* produced in the 1990s brought the life of the nation to a standstill every Sunday morning for many months. It is reported that for many spectators, watching the programme became the equivalent of a visit to the temple as, freshly bathed and dressed in their best clothes, they sat with rapt attention before a television decorated with flowers, to follow the progress of the story. After the programme had ended they broke their ritual fast and went about their daily activities.

Mythological 'comics'

Some thirty years ago, India Book House (Mumbai) initiated an extremely successful series of comic books based around Hindu mythology. These were abridged versions of the great epics and biographies of the core personalities of Indian history and culture. The books were prepared by an excellent team of scholars and researchers with the intention of disseminating knowledge among the masses. Written in English and in most of the eighteen major Indian languages, their layout and images are strongly influenced by the design of Western comics.

India is one of very few countries where mythology still plays a fundamental role in modern life. Ubiquitous throughout India, its present-day imagery has lost none of the vitality of the past, as is demonstrated by the ever-increasing presence of modern religious art and everyday advertisements alluding to mythological incidents. Classical forms have, however, been slightly adjusted to suit modern taste in facial features, costume and colour scheme.

In spite of the dramatic changes within India since independence from colonization, the 'old stories' remain relevant to the majority of the Hindu population, as is evident from the mass appeal of mythological films and television productions of the great epics. Thus, instead of being relegated to a distant past, Hindu myths and their glorious cast of deities remain ever-present in the public view and consciousness.

Suggestions for further reading

A clear explanation of the ideals on which Indian civilization is grounded is given in *Sources of Indian Tradition,* ed. W.T. De Bary (*Introduction to Oriental Civilizations*, New York and London, 1958). T. Richard Blurton's *Hindu Art* (London, 1992 and 2001) is a clear and extremely readable introduction to this absorbing theme.

R.K. Narayan presented a selection of the most famous Hindu myths in *Gods, Demons and Others* (London, 1965), which was followed by his abridged versions of the two great epics of India: *The Ramayana Retold* (London, 1973) and *The Mahabharata Retold* (Mysore, 1978).

On a more specialized level is H. Zimmer's insightful *Myths and Symbols in Indian Art and Civilization* (Princeton, 1953 and 1972) which touches upon the core themes of Hindu mythology and their rendering in art; W. D. O'Flaherty's *Hindu Myths: A Sourcebook Translated from the Sanskrit* (Harmondsworth, 1975) is a wide-ranging selection of myths drawn from Vedic and Puranic literature. *Classical Hindu Mythology: A Reader in the Sanskrit Puranas* (Philadelphia, 1978) is an anthology of texts, compiled by C. Dimmit and J.A.B. van Buitenen.

D.D. Shulman's *Tamil Temple Myths: Sacrifice and Divine Marriage in the South Indian Śaiva Tradition* (Princeton, 1980) is a brilliant study of myths associated with individual temple sites and places them in the context of the Sanskritic Hindu tradition. *Krishna: The Divine Lover: Myth and Legend Through Indian Art* (London and Boston, 1982), ed. A.L. Dallapiccola, studies the complex personality of Krishna. Dallapiccola's *A Dictionary of Hindu Lore and Legend* (London, 2002) explores a number of topics, in particular the complex world of gods, goddesses and semi-divine beings.

Picture credits

Index

References in italics indicate
sources of the myths